IMAGES
of Rail

SOUTHERN PACIFIC RAILROAD IN EASTERN TEXAS

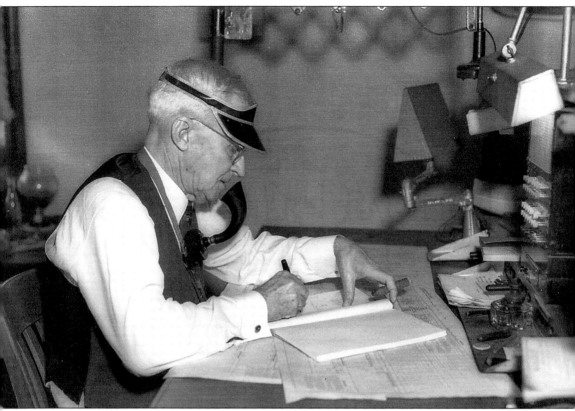

A train dispatcher in Ennis is shown in the process of transmitting a train order to an operator in the early 1950s. He has all the tools of his trade: the large Dispatcher's Record of Train Movements sheet, train order book, message file, and a cigar. Train orders were used to direct train movements in conjunction with the employee timetable. The train dispatcher transmitted them to operators located at stations, who copied them on the prescribed form and repeated them to the dispatcher to insure accuracy. The operators delivered the train orders with a clearance form to the trains. In 1950, Southern Pacific trains in Texas were controlled by train dispatchers located at El Paso, Ennis, Hearne, Houston, Lafayette (Louisiana), San Antonio, Tyler, and Victoria. Train dispatching offices were consolidated beginning with the closure of the Hearne and Victoria offices in 1954. The Tyler office closed in 1958, and its dispatching was transferred to Pine Bluff, Arkansas. In 1959, the remaining offices except Pine Bluff were consolidated into one office in the Southern Pacific Building at 913 Franklin Avenue in Houston. Dispatching was decentralized during 1980 and 1981 with offices at Houston, Lafayette (Louisiana), and Pine Bluff (Arkansas). In 1989, Southern Pacific again centralized train dispatching consolidating the Houston, Kansas City, Lafayette, Pine Bluff, and San Antonio offices into the Eastern Region Transportation Center in Houston. In 1994, the train dispatching moved to Denver, Colorado. Other locations in Texas with SP train dispatching offices were (closing year in parenthesis): Austin (1931), Beaumont (1903), Dallas (1903), Del Rio (1931), Jacksonville (1931), Skidmore (1927), and Yoakum (1925). (Southern Pacific photograph courtesy of John Signor.)

ON THE COVER: The eastbound Hustler is stopped at Ennis in 1953 for passengers, railway express, and to change engine crews. The engineer and fireman worked from Ennis to Dallas on No. 17, the Owl, earlier in the morning and returned to Ennis on No. 16. The Hustler was discontinued on August 11, 1954. (J. Ford Curry courtesy of Dane Williams.)

IMAGES
of Rail

SOUTHERN PACIFIC RAILROAD IN EASTERN TEXAS

David M. Bernstein

ARCADIA
PUBLISHING

Copyright © 2011 by David M. Bernstein
ISBN 978-0-7385-7994-8

Published by Arcadia Publishing
Charleston, South Carolina

Printed in the United States of America

Library of Congress Control Number: 2010940827

For all general information, please contact Arcadia Publishing:
Telephone 843-853-2070
Fax 843-853-0044
E-mail sales@arcadiapublishing.com
For customer service and orders:
Toll-Free 1-888-313-2665

Visit us on the Internet at www.arcadiapublishing.com

Contents

Acknowledgments		6
Introduction		7
Time Line		8
Tables		9
1.	The Hub: Houston Terminal	11
2.	The Houston Division: Houston and Galveston to Echo, Houston to Shreveport	51
3.	The Dallas Division: Houston to Denison, Ennis to Fort Worth	87
Bibliography		127

ACKNOWLEDGMENTS

I wish to thank the following individuals and institutions that contributed photographs for this book: Jimmy Barlow, Gordon Bassett, Barry Byington Jr., John Carr, Carl Codney, Steele Craver, George Hamlin, Tom Kline, Gary Morris, Mike Palmieri, Paul Sartori, Jim Shaw, John Signor, Southern Pacific Transportation Company, Steve Standifer, Harold Vollrath, Dane Williams, California State Railroad Museum (Sacramento, California), and Railroad and Heritage Museum (Temple, Texas).

A special thank-you to Craig Order, archivist at the Railroad and Heritage Museum in Temple, for providing unlimited access to the Dean Hale and Joe R. Thompson photographic collections. The museum was kind enough to permit use of many images from their collection. It is possible some of the photographs credited to Dean Hale may have been taken by other photographers and incorporated into Dean's collection, as the record in Dean's notes are not clear on this matter.

The reference material used in preparation for this book is primarily from my extensive historical archive. I wish to thank the Rollin Bredenberg for providing me unlimited access to Southern Pacific's records stored in the Topek Building in Houston, many boxes of which reside in my archives. I also wish to thank Art Henson for allowing me access to the Southern Pacific General Managers records file room at the Southern Pacific Building in Houston. The hundreds of pages from documents copied from those files provided much of the historical information presented. Bill Neill provided access to his collection of timetables, documents, and employee magazines, which were invaluable in preparing this book.

INTRODUCTION

This book is a photographic record of the Southern Pacific's Houston and Dallas Divisions from the end of World War II through the merger with the Union Pacific Railroad in 1996. The term "divisions" refers to the operating divisions defined in 1946 and the geographic coverage is depicted on the map on page 10. The Houston terminals were used by the Dallas, Houston, and San Antonio Divisions. This book is not intended to be a detailed corporate or operational history, but rather an insight to the railroad during the last five decades of its operation in Texas.

Southern Pacific and its predecessor companies operated in Texas for 143 years. The first line constructed was the Buffalo Bayou, Brazos and Colorado Railway Company (incorporated in 1850), which constructed 81 miles westward from Harrisburg to Columbus from 1853 to 1866. This was the first railroad constructed in Texas, the first constructed west of the Mississippi River at the standard gauge of 4 feet 8½ inches between rails, and the oldest corporate predecessor of what became the Southern Pacific. The original Southern Pacific Company was incorporated 1865 in California as a land holding company, and on September 25, 1868, it was purchased by a group of four investors who owned the Central Pacific Railroad. In 1881, Southern Pacific, both as a corporation and individually by Collis P. Huntington, began purchasing railroad companies in Texas and Louisiana. These companies were leased to a new Southern Pacific Company incorporated in 1885. The Union Pacific and Southern Pacific were under common ownership from 1901 until 1913 when the U.S. Supreme Court ordered Union Pacific to divest all of its Southern Pacific stock.

There were 62 individual railroad companies that comprised Southern Pacific's lines in Texas. By 1946, the corporate structure had been streamlined into five companies:

- The Texas & New Orleans Railroad: 3,634 miles of railroad in Texas. Merged into the Southern Pacific Company in 1961.
- The St. Louis Southwestern Railway Company of Texas (Cotton Belt): 854 miles of railroad in Texas. Acquired by Southern Pacific in 1932. Merged with Union Pacific Railroad in 1996.
- The Southern Pacific Terminal Company: 22 miles of trackage in Galveston. Merged into the Texas & New Orleans Railroad in 1960.
- The El Paso & Southwestern Railroad Company Of Texas: 18 miles in the El Paso area. Merged into the Southern Pacific Company in 1961.
- The Texas State Railroad: 35 miles between Rusk and Palestine operated under lease 1920–1963.

In 1969, Southern Pacific's railroad properties became the Southern Pacific Transportation Company. The non-railroad subsidiaries of the Southern Pacific Company merged with the Santa Fe Industries in 1984. The Interstate Commerce Commission rejected the merger with the Atchison, Topeka & Santa Fe Railway in 1986, and the Southern Pacific Transportation Company operated independently until the 1988 purchased by Rio Grande Industries, owners of the Denver & Rio Grande Western Railroad, to form Southern Pacific Rail Corporation. Southern Pacific merged with the Union Pacific Railroad in September 1996.

Southern Pacific headquarters was located on Market Street in San Francisco, California. There was a vice president headquartered at the Southern Pacific Building in Houston, and the Texas and Louisiana lines operated with autonomy until the early 1970s. General governance was exercised from San Francisco, but most of the daily functions of the railroad were directed from Houston. The St. Louis Southwestern Railway (Cotton Belt) maintained the same relationship with corporate headquarters until 1975.

TIME LINE

January 1853 • Construction of the Houston to Dallas line began in Houston.
January 1861 • Texas & New Orleans Railroad completed 105-mile line between Houston and Orange.
July 1876 • Construction of the Houston East & West Texas Railway narrow gauge line to Shreveport commenced in Houston.
July 1872 • The Houston & Texas Central Railway line from Houston reached Dallas.
March 1873 • Completion of the Houston & Texas Central line at Denison.
August 30, 1880 • Through passenger train service commenced between Houston and New Orleans.
January 7, 1883 • Completion of the Sunset Route between Los Angeles and New Orleans at Eagles Nest, 227 miles west of San Antonio.
February 5, 1883 • Through passenger train service commenced between Los Angeles and New Orleans.
December 8, 1886 • Completion of the line between Fort Worth and Garrett.
January 26, 1889 • Through passenger train service commenced between Houston and Shreveport.
July 29, 1894 • The entire line between Houston and Shreveport was converted from narrow gauge to standard gauge in a single day.
1898 • The final segment of the line between Houston and Galveston was completed.
July 1901 • Southern Pacific began conversion of steam locomotives from coal to oil fuel.
December 16, 1906 • Completion of the 94-mile cut off between Nelleva Junction and Mexia.
May 11, 1911 • The Owl commenced operation between Dallas and Houston.
October 14, 1916 • Dallas Union Station opened for business.
September 12, 1920 • The Dallas Belt line opened between Forest Avenue and T&P Junction.
May 1, 1926 • Southern Pacific obtained control of the Dayton–Goose Creek Railway.
April 1, 1928 • Southern Pacific acquired the Texas Midland Railroad (Ennis to Paris).
January 12, 1932 • The Interstate Commerce Commission approved Southern Pacific's acquisition of the St. Louis Southwestern Railway (Cotton Belt Route), effective April 1932.
May 8, 1933 • Abandonment of the 94-mile Nelleva Junction–Mexia Cut Off.
September 1, 1934 • Grand Central Station in Houston opened for business.
December 16, 1935 • Passenger service ended between Dallas and Denison.
September 19, 1937 • The Sunbeam was equipped with streamlined equipment.
April 1941 • The Texas & New Orleans Railroad received its first diesel locomotive.
February 1946 • The Blue Streak Merchandise freight train began transcontinental operation between East St. Louis to Los Angeles via Corsicana.
April 8, 1950 • The Sunset Limited was reequipped with new 15-car streamlined train sets.
August 4, 1951 • Passenger service between Houston and Galveston ended.
May 4, 1953 • The piggyback (trailer of flat car) era began on Southern Pacific with the inauguration of service between Houston and New Orleans.
October 1953 • Construction began on the Englewood hump yard in Houston.
August 11, 1954 • The Hustler was discontinued between Houston and Dallas.
September 11, 1955 • The final runs of the Sunbeam between Houston and Dallas.
January 25, 1957 • The last Texas & New Orleans Railroad steam locomotive, No. 822, was retired.
June 8, 1959 • Passenger service ended between Houston and Dallas with discontinuance of the Owl.
November 26, 1959 • The new Houston passenger station opened, replacing Grand Central Station.
May 1, 1971 • Amtrak assumed operation of the Sunset Limited.
September 21, 1974 • Massive explosion and fire at Englewood Yard caused by a ruptured tank car.
July 24, 1986 • The Interstate Commerce Commission denied the merger between the Southern Pacific Transportation Company and the Atchison, Topeka & Santa Fe Railway.
April 4, 1988 • Sale of 34 miles of railroad right of way to Dallas Area Rapid Transit for $38 million.
October 13, 1988 • Rio Grande Industries purchased the Southern Pacific Transportation Co.
September 11, 1996 • The Interstate Commerce Commission approved the merger of the Union Pacific Railroad and the Southern Pacific Rail Corporation.

Southern Pacific Houston Division • Lines in Operation 1946

Subdivision	Between	Miles	Constructed	Disposition
Beaumont	Houston and Echo	111	1858–1870	Active (Union Pacific Railroad).
Lufkin	Houston and Lufkin	117	1876–1882	Active (Union Pacific Railroad).
Shreveport	Lufkin and Shreveport, LA	115	1882–1885	Active (Union Pacific Railroad).
Galveston	Houston and Galveston	57	1876–1892	Seabrook to San Leon abandoned in 1996. Remainder active (Union Pacific Railroad).
Jacksonville	Dallas and Jacksonville	113	1880–1902	Jacksonville to Seagoville abandoned in 1981. Seagoville to Elam abandoned in 1989. Elam to Briggs (Dallas) sold to DART (Dallas Area Rapid Transit) 1988 and abandoned by DART in 1999.
Rockland	Jacksonville and Beaumont	168	1881–1903	Dunagan to Nacogdoches abandoned 1957. Beaumont to Loeb Jct. abandoned in 1961. Loeb Jct. to Hillister abandoned in 1991. Hillister to Dolan abandoned in 1993. Dolan to Dunagan sold to Angelina & Neches River in 1994.
Sabine	Beaumont and Port Arthur	21	1880–1881	Active (Union Pacific Railroad).
Paris	Kaufman and Paris	94	1894–1896	Kaufman to Greenville abandoned in 1958. Commerce to Paris abandoned in 1975 (service discontinued October 20, 1971). Trackage in Paris abandoned in 1984.
Baytown	Dayton and Baytown	25	1917–1919	Active (Union Pacific Railroad).
Palestine	Rusk and Palestine (Texas State Railroad)	33	1893–1909	Southern Pacific leased the Texas State Railroad from 1921 until October 31, 1962.

The Galveston Subdivision was abandoned between Pasadena Jct. and Deer Park Jct. in 1961 and the right of way used for construction of the Pasadena Freeway. A new line was constructed.
The Galveston Subdivision was abandoned in 1964 between Buffalo Bayou and Manchester, Southern Pacific operating over trackage owned by the Port Terminal Railroad Association after the abandonment.
The Beaumont Subdivision was abandoned between Beaumont and Tower 31 in 1967.

Southern Pacific Dallas Division • Lines in Operation 1946

Subdivision	Between	Miles	Constructed	Disposition
Denison	Denison and Ennis	107	1872–1873	Active between Denison and Allen and between former
	Dallas and T. & P. Jct.	5	1918–1921	T. & P. Jct. and Ennis.
	T. & P. Jct. and Gifford	9	1924–1926	See note following this table.
Ennis	Ennis and Hearne	110	1869–1872	Active (Union Pacific Railroad).
Hearne	Hearne and Houston	121	1853–1869	Active (Union Pacific Railroad).
Fort Worth	Fort Worth and Garrett	53	1875–1886	Active (Union Pacific Railroad).
Waco	Bremond and Waco	44	1872	Abandoned in 1965. Trackage between Waco and Marlin sold to Missouri Pacific Railroad.

Denison to South Sherman Jct. was sold to Burlington Northern Railroad in 1991.
South Sherman Jct. to Spring Creek Parkway Plano was leased to the Dallas, Garland & Northeastern Railroad in 1999, sold to Dallas Area Rapid Transit in 2001 and abandoned south of Allen in 2006.
Spring Creek Parkway Plano to M. P. Junction (formerly T. & P. Junction) was sold to Dallas Area Rapid Transit in 1988.

Discontinuance Dates of Selected Passenger Trains

Railroad	Trains	Name	Between	Discontinued
S. P.	39 • 40	Passenger	Ennis and Paris	May 11, 1941
S. P.	82 • 83	Passenger	Ennis and Fort Worth	August 24, 1941
S. P.	65 • 66	Mixed train	Bremond and Waco	August 16, 1949
S. P.	42 • 43	Passenger	Houston and Austin	November 19, 1949
S. P.	171 • 172	Passenger	Houston and Galveston	August 4, 1951
S. P.	45 • 46	Passenger	Houston and Austin	December 9, 1951
S. P.	85 • 86	Passenger	Ennis and Fort Worth	December 27, 1951
S. P.	155 • 156	Mixed train	Dallas and Beaumont via Jacksonville and Kountze	August 1, 1952
S. P.	7 • 8	Alamo	Houston and New Orleans, Louisiana	December 27, 1952
S. P.	25 • 26	Passenger	Houston and Logansport, Louisiana	August 4, 1954
S. P.	25 • 26	Passenger	Logansport and Shreveport, Louisiana	August 9, 1954
S. P.	15 • 16	Hustler	Houston and Dallas	August 11, 1954
S. P.	13 • 14	Sunbeam	Houston and Dallas	September 12, 1955
S. P.	27 • 28	Passenger	Houston and Shreveport	September 29, 1955
S. P.	3 • 4	Acadian	Houston and Echo	September 30, 1956
S. P.	17 • 18	Owl	Houston and Dallas	June 8, 1958
S. P.	5 • 6	Argonaut	Houston and New Orleans, Louisiana	September 24, 1963
S. P.	1 • 2	Sunset Limited	Los Angeles and New Orleans (reduced to triweekly)	October 1, 1970
Amtrak	521 • 522	Eagle	Houston and Dallas	September 11, 1995

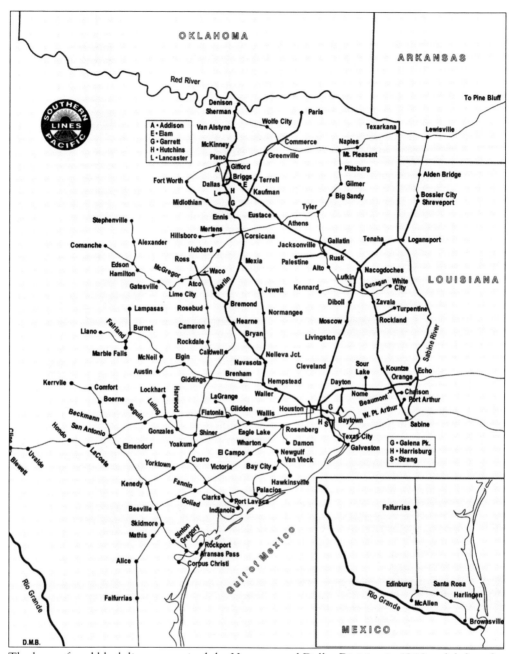

The heavy-faced black lines comprised the Houston and Dallas Division in 1946 and define the scope of this book. The heavy-faced gray lines were part of the Houston and Dallas Divisions abandoned prior to 1946 (abandonment year in parenthesis):

Hutchins to Lancaster (1924)
Rockland to Turpentine (1927)
W. Port Arthur to Sabine (1931)

Commerce to Greenville (1933)
Nelleva Jct. to Mexica Jct. (1933)
Nome to Sour Lake (1933)

Gallatin to Rusk (1934)
Ennis to Kaufman (1942)

The light-faced lines are other lines operated by Southern Pacific.

One

THE HUB
HOUSTON TERMINAL

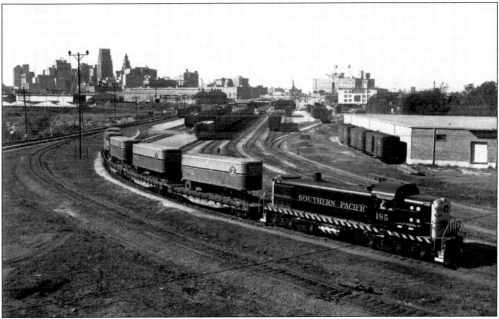

Brand new Alco RSD-5 engine number 185 has five trailers-on-flat cars (TOFC) near Semmes Junction at Houston in 1953. The track curving in the foreground is the Lufkin Subdivision main track. Immediately behind the photographer is the main line to New Orleans. The yard served the Houston Freight Station at San Jacinto Street visible in the background, which employed 120 people and handled a monthly average of 25 million pounds of freight in 1956. Opened for business in 1926 and substantially rehabilitated in 1956, the station had 137,750 square feet of floor space, 28,000 feet of track, and space for 120 trucks. Most of the freight handled at the freight station was the less-than-carload (LCL) merchandise for 6,500 regular monthly customers that arrived in freight cars, and much of it was distributed to customers by trucking subsidiary Southern Pacific Transport Company. (Southern Pacific courtesy of John Signor.)

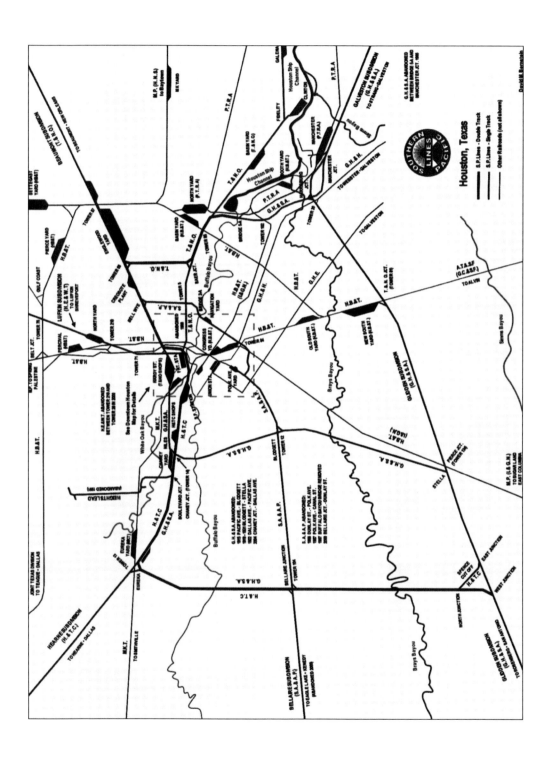

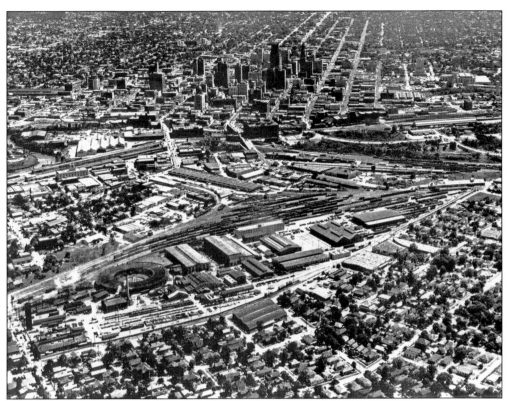

This aerial view of downtown Houston was taken in 1951 looking southward. The foreground is dominated by Southern Pacific's Hardy Street locomotive shop complex and freight yard. The map below depicts the railroad facilities in the downtown area in 1950. Facilities labeled Texas & New Orleans (T&NO) are Southern Pacific. (Above, Southern Pacific courtesy of John Signor; Below, David M. Bernstein.)

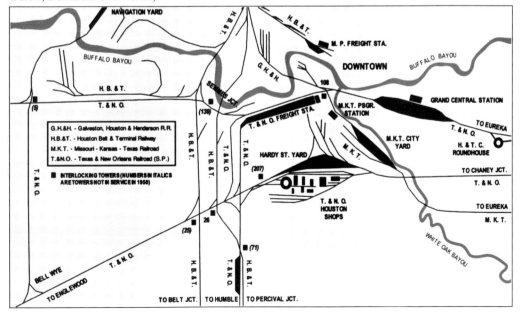

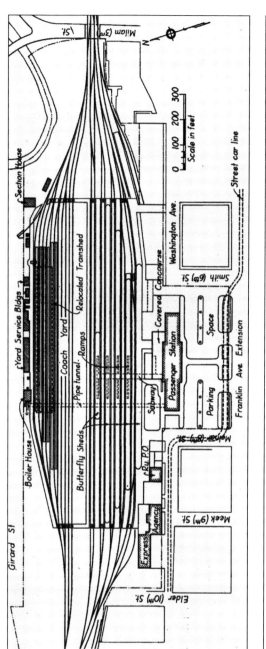 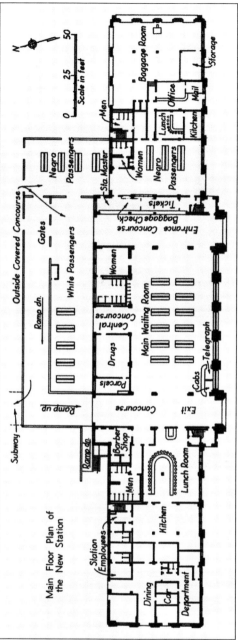

Grand Central Station in Houston was formally opened on September 14, 1934, after two years of construction. Built at a cost of $3.5 million (equivalent to approximately $57 million in 2010), it replaced the old six-track Houston & Texas Central Railroad station constructed in 1888. The four-story station accommodated passenger facilities including ticketing, waiting rooms, lunchroom, barbershop, baggage facilities, and station offices. The Houston Division superintendent's office and train dispatching office occupied the second floor and records storage on the third floor. The Houston Model Railroad Club occupied the fourth floor with a 70-by-30-foot layout, attracting about 6,500 visitors during their annual open house. (Diagrams from *Railway Age* Magazine, October 20, 1934.)

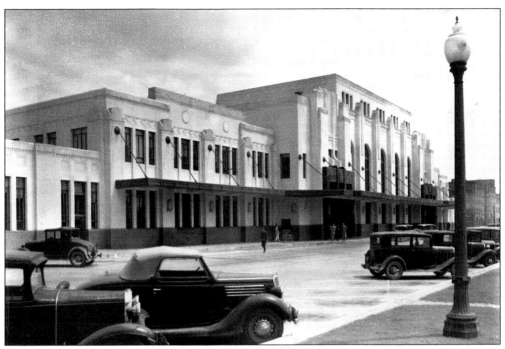

These photographs showcase the exterior and interior of the handsome art deco Grand Central Station in Houston. The main waiting room featured a 41-foot ceiling and mural of Sam Houston. (Southern Pacific.)

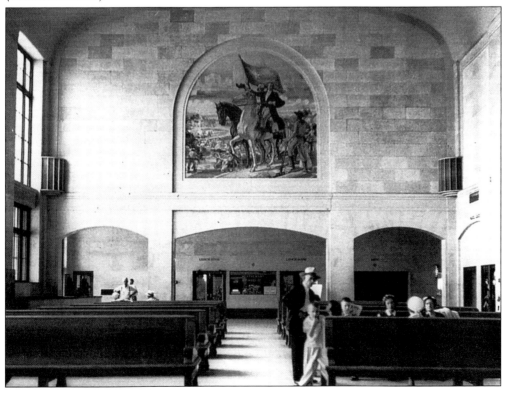

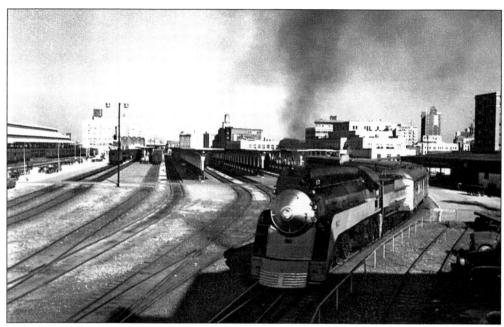

Grand Central Station had a total of 21 tracks, including 10 station tracks, two through tracks and nine coach yard tracks. The large car shed in the left side of the photograph was the original 600-foot-long-by-95-foot-wide six-track passenger shed from the original 1888 station that was dismantled and moved to the new coach yard. The Sunbeam is departing from Track No. 1 en route to Dallas on August 9, 1953. (Roger S. Plummer courtesy of Gordon Bassett.)

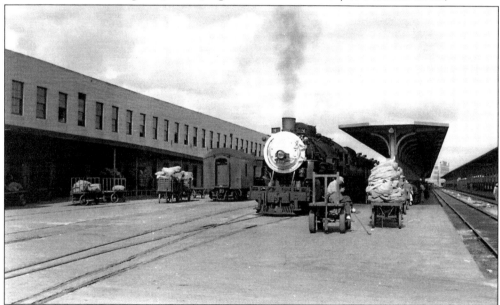

Grand Central Station featured a covered 46-foot-wide-by-187-foot-long outside concourse between the building and the tracks with passenger seating and gates. The station handled large quantities of express and mail traffic, exemplified in this photograph taken in 1952 with Train No. 26 preparing to depart for Shreveport, Louisiana. (Joe R. Thompson courtesy of the Railroad and Heritage Museum Temple, Texas.)

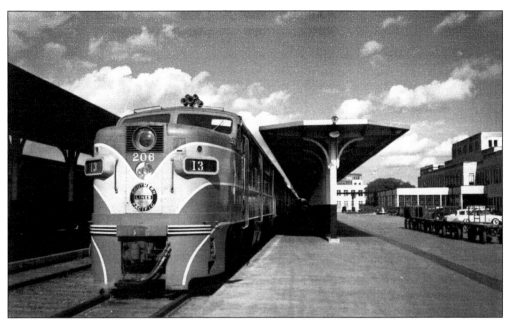

Train No. 13, the Dallas-bound Sunbeam, occupies its customary spot on Track No. 1 at Houston's Grand Central Station in this c. 1953 image. Visible in the background is the outside covered concourse between the station building and tracks. The Houston Division train dispatching office occupied the second floor of the station until it was moved to the Southern Pacific Building at 913 Franklin Avenue in 1959. (Joe R. Thompson courtesy of the Railroad and Heritage Museum, Temple, Texas.)

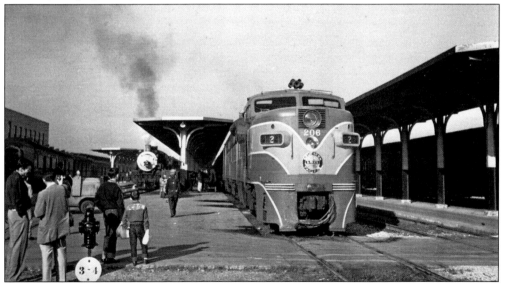

Train No. 2, the eastbound Sunset Limited, is preparing for its 8:40 a.m. departure from Grand Central Station to New Orleans with stops at Beaumont, Orange, Lake Charles, and Lafayette. The extra fare Sunset Limited between Los Angeles and New Orleans was streamlined in 1951 with new 15-car train sets consisting of sleeping cars, a full lounge car with a shower and bath, chair cars, dining car, and coffee shop lounge car. (Joe R. Thompson courtesy of the Railroad and Heritage Museum, Temple, Texas.)

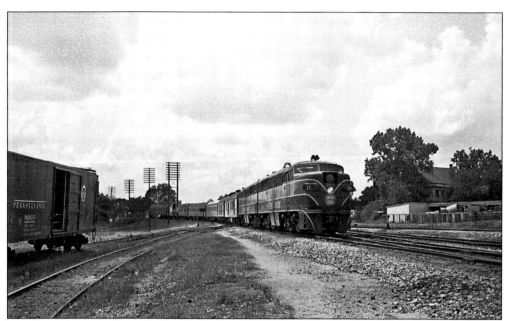

The six-car Hustler arrives Houston from Dallas in 1953. This photograph was taken at the west end of the passenger station looking westward, the same location as the photographs on the next page. The Hustler offered early morning departures in both directions, making 11 regular stops and 15 flag stops en route with a running time just under six hours. (Joe R. Thompson courtesy of the Railroad and Heritage Museum, Temple, Texas.)

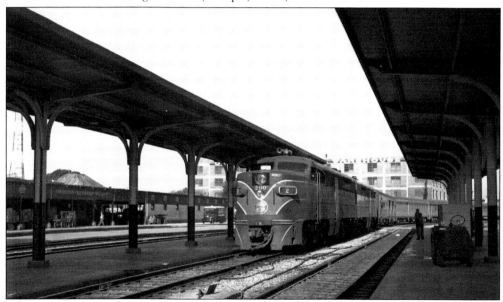

The Los Angeles to New Orleans streamlined Sunset Limited arriving Houston Grand Central Station in 1953. Southern Pacific inaugurated passenger service between California and New Orleans on February 3, 1883. The Sunset Limited began as a one day per week train between San Francisco and New Orleans on November 1, 1894. It operated on various weekly, biweekly, and triweekly schedules until daily operation began on November 11, 1902. (Joe R. Thompson courtesy Railroad and Heritage Museum, Temple, Texas.)

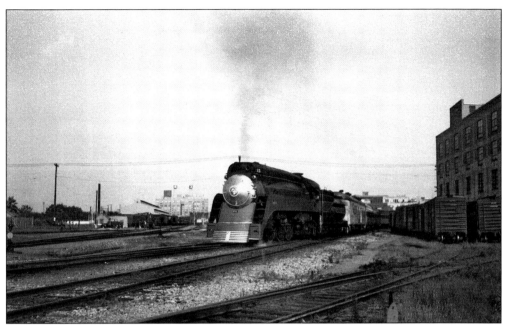

The Sunbeam began service as a six-and-a-half-hour express train between Houston and Dallas on September 6, 1925, which was one hour faster than the fastest train on this route. The only stop was at Ennis to change crews and offer Fort Worth passengers connecting service. On September 19, 1937, a new streamlined Sunbeam service was introduced on a 4-hour, 45-minute schedule operating at a maximum speed of 80 miles per hour. Two eight-car stainless-steel streamlined train sets were constructed consisting of a baggage car, 48-seat coach, four 50-seat articulated coaches, a 32-seat parlor car and a 46-seat diner/lounge/observation car. Each train set had a total seating capacity of 326 passengers. These photographs document the afternoon departure of Train No. 13, the northbound Sunbeam, from Houston's Grand Central Station during 1953. The boxcars in the right margin are spotted at the Union Terminal Warehouse Company. (Joe R. Thompson courtesy of the Railroad and Heritage Museum, Temple, Texas.)

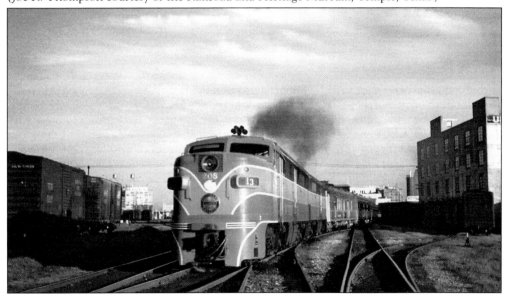

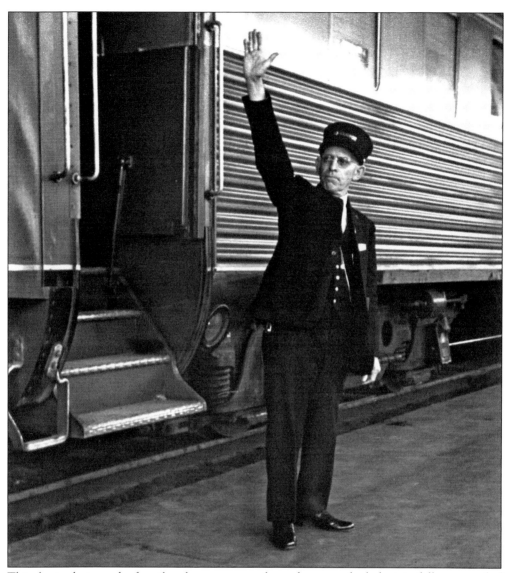

This classic photograph of a railroad passenger conductor leaves no doubt he is in full command of his train. Conductor S. R. Curry of Ennis is at Houston's Grand Central Station on the Sunbeam as it prepares for its 4:45 p.m. departure to Dallas. The date is June 30, 1954, and Mr. Curry is making his final run closing out a 52-year railroad career where he logged 2,400,038 miles as a brakeman and conductor in freight and passenger service. When he began his career in 1907, a fast passenger train made the run between Houston and Dallas in 10 hours. On this day in 1954, the Sunbeam will cover the 265-mile run in 4 hours and 25 minutes with only a flag stop in College Station and a brief stop at Ennis to change engine crews and discharge passengers. (J. Ford Curry courtesy of Dane Williams.)

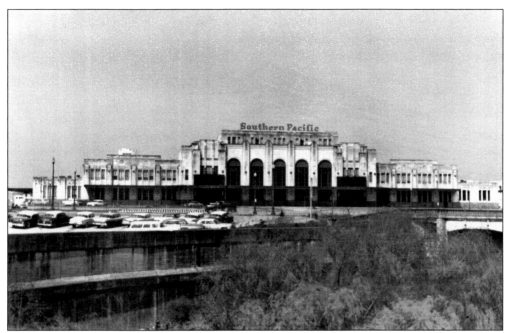

Houston Grand Central Station in 1959 shortly before its demolition. The station exclusively served Southern Pacific trains, although the Missouri–Kansas–Texas Railroad (MKT) inquired about using the station for their trains in 1941, 1945, and 1950. Southern Pacific feared possible loss of mail and express business to the MKT would not be offset by rental charges and declined their requests. (Joe R. Thompson courtesy of the Railroad and Heritage Museum, Temple, Texas.)

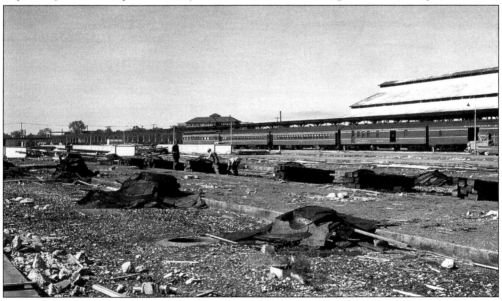

Most of the land occupied by Houston's Grand Central Station was sold to the General Services Administration for construction of a U.S. post office in 1959. The station was in service for only 25 years before being replaced by a modest two-platform facility. When Grand Central Station opened in 1934, it served 28 trains each day, but by 1959, it was serving only four trains per day. (Joe R. Thompson courtesy of the Railroad and Heritage Museum Temple, Texas.)

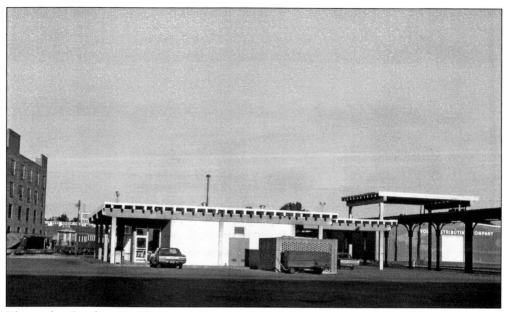

The modest Southern Pacific Houston passenger station which replaced Grand Central Station following its demolition in 1959. All that remained from the original station was two passenger tracks and one platform. The station is now owned by the National Railroad Passenger Corporation and serves Amtrak trains. (Joe R. Thompson courtesy of the Railroad and Heritage Museum, Temple, Texas.)

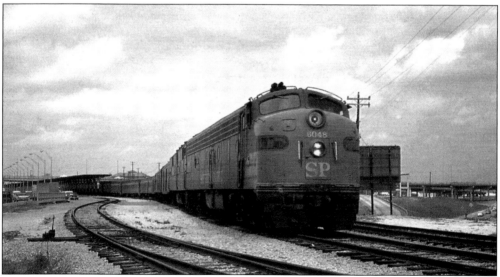

The eastward Sunset Limited is departing the Houston passenger station, in this c. 1965 image. The competition for passengers by auto and air travel and the loss of mail and express business forced reduction in service at Houston from 30 trains per day in 1949 to two trains per day in 1963. During the 1960s, the Sunset Limited lost its dining car and sleeping car services, relegating it to a coach train with an automatic buffet car for meals. On November 1, 1970, dining car and sleeping car service was reestablished and service reduced to three days per week in each direction. Amtrak assumed operation of the Sunset Limited on May 1, 1971. (Joe R. Thompson courtesy of the Railroad and Heritage Museum, Temple, Texas.)

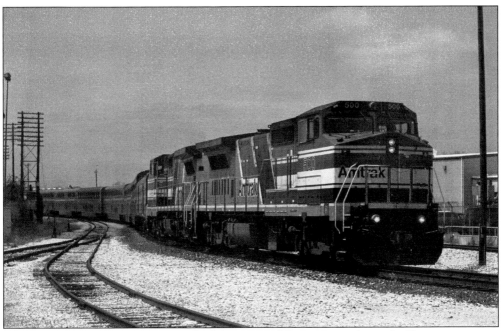

Two Amtrak P32-8BWH locomotives lead the eastward Sunset Limited into the Houston passenger station on April 6, 1993. Other Amtrak trains that served the former Southern Pacific station were the Lone Star (August 1, 1974 to October 9, 1979), Inter-American (October 10, 1979 to September 30, 1981) and Texas Eagle (November 15, 1988 to September 10, 1995). (George W. Hamlin.)

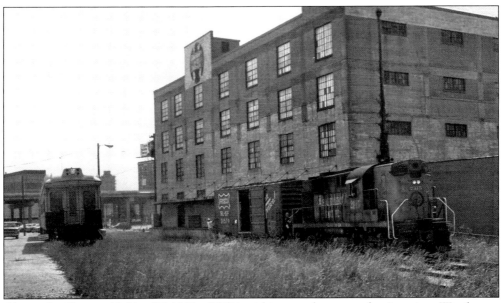

Above, the 19-year-old Alco RS-11 No. 2915 is picking up a boxcar at the American Warehouse, adjacent to the Houston passenger station in October 1978. This is the same location featured in the photographs on page 19. Parked in the spur is Southern Pacific Business Car No. 127, the Alamo, which was assigned to the Houston Division superintendent. The Alamo served SP officials for 56 years from 1926 until 1982. (Gary Morris.)

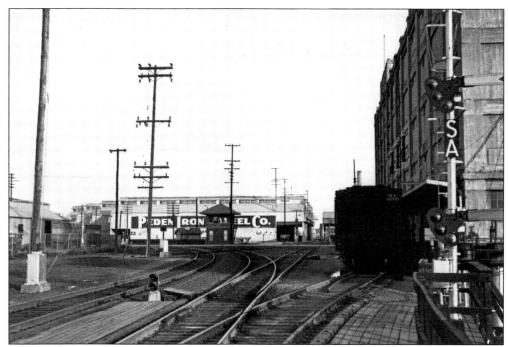

Viewed from the White Oak Bayou Bridge is Tower 108, approximately one half mile east of Grand Central Station. The two tracks curving to the left are Southern Pacific's line to Tower 26. The Missouri–Kansas–Texas Railroad is visible crossing the SP line in front of the tower. The road crossing in front of the tower is San Jacinto Street. (Joe R. Thompson courtesy of the Railroad and Heritage Museum, Temple, Texas.)

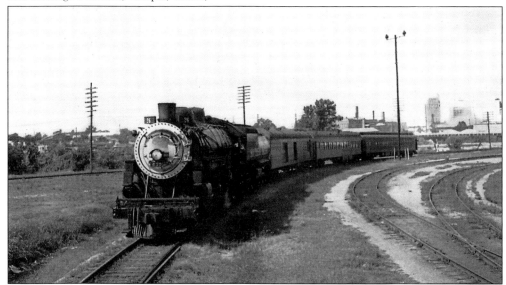

Train No. 26, en route to Lufkin and Shreveport, is passing the yard tracks for the Houston Freight Station in this 1953 photograph. For many years, passenger service on this line consisted of daytime trains 25 and 26, with coaches and overnight trains 27 and 28 handling coaches and sleeping cars. From 1932 to 1937, the night trains were operated as mixed trains carrying passengers and freight. (Joe R. Thompson courtesy of the Railroad and Heritage Museum, Temple, Texas.)

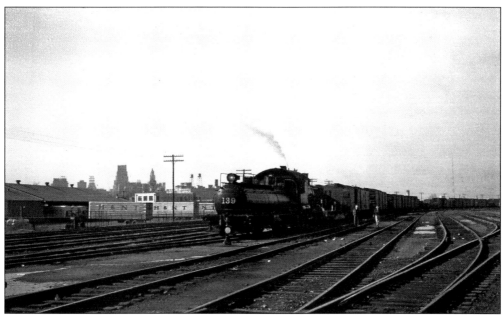

Presented here are two views of the Hardy Street Yard during the mid-1950s. Above, Southern Pacific Class S-13 locomotive 139 is switching a large string of freight cars at the west end of the yard. No. 139 was built in December 1920 by Baldwin Locomotive Works and was scrapped on August 21, 1956, in Houston. Below, Extra 320 West en route to Englewood Yard passes steam and diesel switch engines working the yard. Hardy Street Yard was the original Texas & New Orleans Railroad yard in Houston, constructed as Fifth Ward Yard in the late 1860s. The Galveston, Harrisburg & San Antonio Railway also used this yard. Englewood Yard was built in 1895, and following its expansion in 1913, became the primary classification yard, with Hardy Street relegated to switching local industry cars effective November 15, 1914. In 1955, Hardy Street Yard had 23 tracks with aggregate length of 52,252 feet. (Joe R. Thompson courtesy Railroad and Heritage Museum, Temple, Texas.)

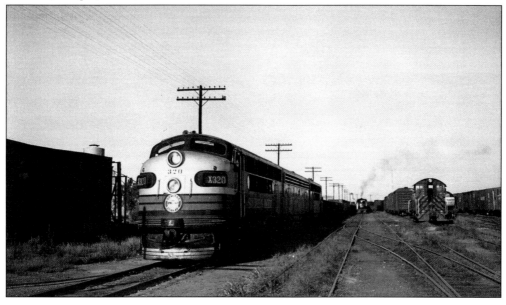

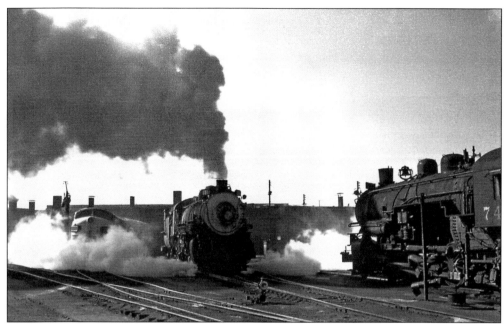

Southern Pacific No. 749 exhausts steam as it gets underway at Hardy Street Shops during its last year of service in 1954. The sister Class Mk-5 Mikado locomotive to the right waits for transfer to Commercial Metals in Houston for scrapping. The Hardy Street Shops were constructed by the Texas & New Orleans Railroad in the 1860s. The shops were expanded in 1887 to accommodate the Galveston, Harrisburg & San Antonio Railway, which closed their shops at Harrisburg in January 1888. (Joe R. Thompson courtesy of the Railroad and Heritage Museum, Temple, Texas.)

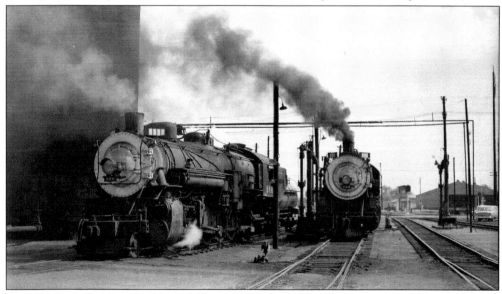

Class F-1 Santa Fe Type No. 986 and Class Mk-5 Mikado Type 786 pose at the east end of Hardy Street Shops around 1954. No. 986 was a truly massive locomotive with a 2-10-2 wheel arrangement and weighing 353,000 pounds. It was sold for scrap to Houston Compressed Steel on March 25, 1955. No. 786 escaped scrapping and was donated to the City of Austin in 1956. (Joe R. Thompson courtesy of the Railroad and Heritage Museum, Temple, Texas.)

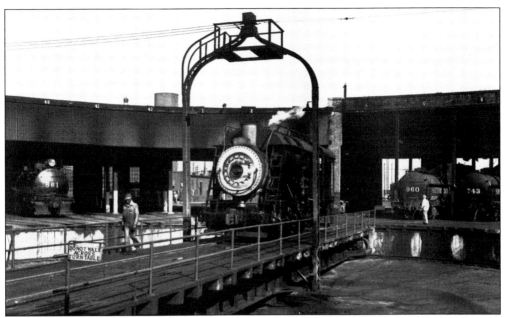

MW 3230 served as the Hardy Street Shop Switcher from 1947 until 1956. It was built in 1911 by Baldwin Locomotive Works and began service as standard 0-6-0 switch engine No. 102 with a tender. On July 3, 1947, it was rebuilt as a saddle tank engine for shop switching and renumbered MW 3230 (the maintenance-of-way prefix was used to distinguish it from a revenue service engine). It was sold for scrap on September 12, 1956. (Joe R. Thompson courtesy of the Railroad and Heritage Museum, Temple, Texas.)

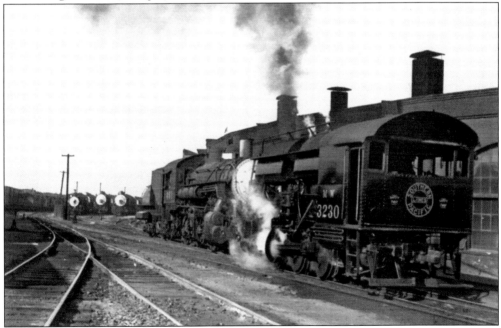

The Hardy Street Shop Switcher MW 3230 is shown hostling Mikado 2-8-2 No. 461 outside the shops. The 3230 is manned by a hostler who was restricted to moving locomotives in the shop area. (Joe R. Thompson courtesy of the Railroad and Heritage Museum, Temple, Texas.)

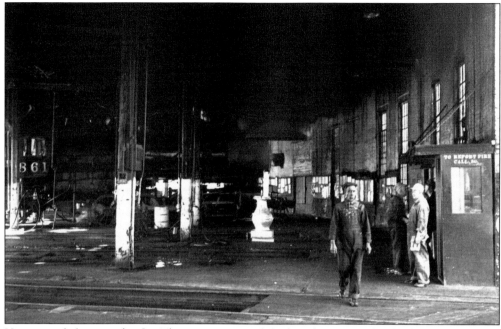

Houston rail photographer Joe Thompson captured the less glamorous side of railroading at Hardy Street. Dirty, hot, and humid in the summer and cold and damp in the winter, the Hardy Street Shops built and maintained locomotives for over a century. (Courtesy of Railroad and Heritage Museum, Temple, Texas.)

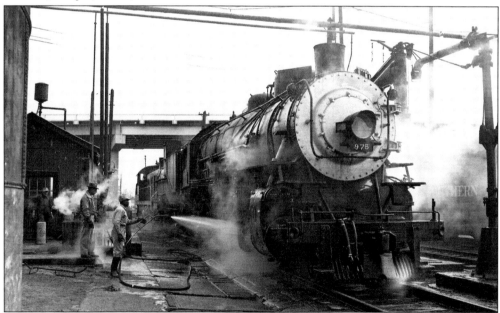

Santa Fe Type No. 975 received cleaning from high-pressure hoses at Hardy Street in Houston on a gloomy day in the early 1950s. The massive 2-10-2 locomotive was built by Baldwin Locomotive Works in 1918 and served Southern Pacific for 39 years. She was donated to the City of Beaumont on February 2, 1957, and today resides at the Illinois Railway Museum in Union, Illinois. (Joe R. Thompson courtesy of the Railroad and Heritage Museum, Temple, Texas.)

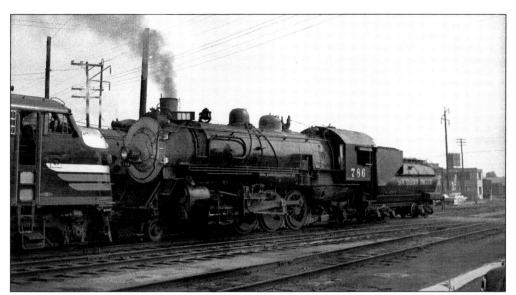

Southern Pacific 786 spends time during a layover at Hardy Street Shops between assignments. Five engines of the 700 series were donated to cities in Texas for preservation. No. 786 was donated to the city of Austin on March 24, 1956, and spent the next 34 years as a static display. In 1989, the city donated the locomotive to the Austin Steam Train Association and the $1-million restoration to service began in June 1990 at Georgetown, Texas. No. 786 pulled its first excursion train between Cedar Park and Burnet on July 25, 1992. (Joe R. Thompson courtesy of the Railroad and Heritage Museum, Temple, Texas.)

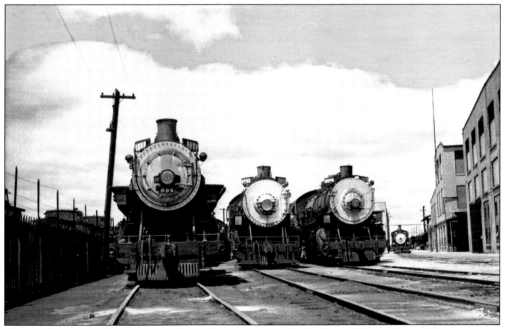

Above, three steam locomotives share idle time at the Hardy Street Shops. From left to right are 2-6-0 Mogul No. 696 scrapped September 4, 1953, 2-8-2 Mikado No. 777 sold for scrap February 8, 1955, and sister No. 740 sold for scrap June 15, 1954. (Joe R. Thompson courtesy of the Railroad and Heritage Museum, Temple.)

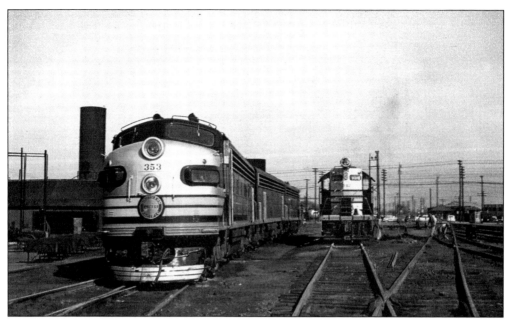

The east end of Hardy Street Shops was a busy place on the day this photograph was taken in 1954. A 4,500-horsepower diesel consist with F3A No. 353 and two other units is accompanied by brand new 1,750-horsepower GP-9 locomotive No. 242 on the center track. A maintenance-of-way gang is performing track maintenance on the lead track. (Joe R. Thompson courtesy of the Railroad and Heritage Museum, Temple, Texas.)

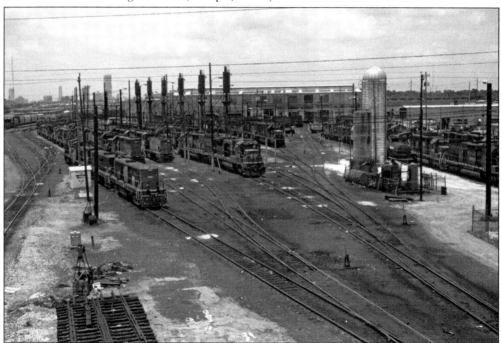

This is a west facing view of the diesel sanding, oiling, and fuel facilities at Hardy Street in the 1980s with downtown Houston looming in the background. The shop buildings, servicing facilities, and most of the yard no longer exist. (Tom Kline.)

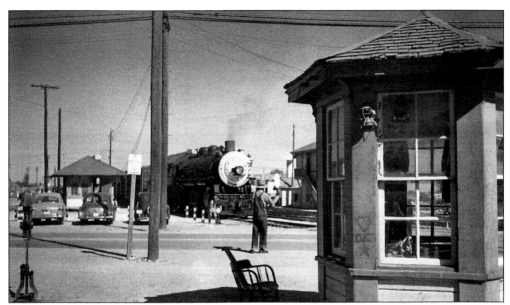

The crossing watchman at Hardy Street has vacated his rocking chair in the shade of the shanty to halt traffic for the passage of an eastward train by using a stop sign and whistle. This was the only crossing in Houston protected by watchmen in the 1950s, with the exception of temporary watchman employed during construction of the Lockwood Avenue overpass. In 1956, Southern Pacific employed 32 crossing watchmen to protect 11 crossings in Texas. (Joe R. Thompson courtesy of Railroad and Heritage Museum, Temple, Texas.)

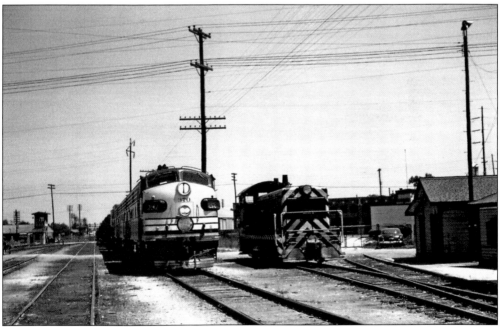

Train No. 357 en route to Denison is crossing Elysian Street with F7A locomotive 370 on the point passes Alco S-2 switch engine 70 occupying the Norvell-Wilder lead track. The industry track curving to the right served Standard Oil Supply Company. (Joe R. Thompson courtesy of the Railroad and Heritage Museum, Temple, Texas.)

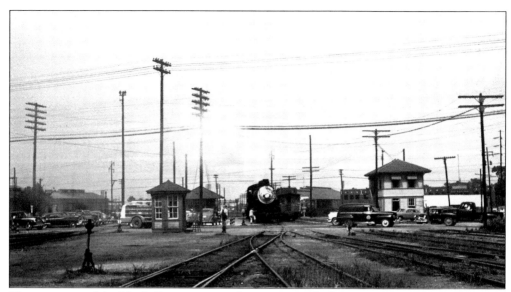

This is a view of the Hardy Street crossing facing west with the crossing watchman's shanty in the left center. Hardy Street was a major thoroughfare prior to completion of the Elysian Street Viaduct in 1956. Due to the complexity of the track layout, frequent train movements, and heavy vehicle traffic, it was not practical to install flashers and gates here until the early 1960s. Timetable special instructions until 1962 required "train and engine movements must approach Hardy Street with caution, prepared to stop if necessary to avoid accident." (Joe R. Thompson courtesy of the Railroad and Heritage Museum, Temple, Texas.)

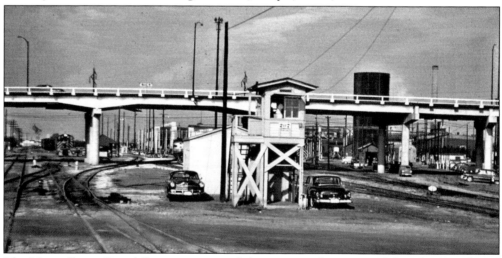

The Maury Street Signal Operator occupied the tower in the center of this photograph and controlled the crossing gates at Maury Street and the Centralized Traffic Control installed in 1942 on the single track freight line between the west end of Tower 26 interlocking limits and Niles. In 1956, the tower was designated as Tower 207 and the interlocking at the east end of Hardy Street was transferred from Tower 26 to Tower 207. In 1959, there was a rearrangement of tracks and the abolishment of switch engines at Hardy Street, after which Tower 207 was closed and Tower 26 assumed its functions. This photograph is a westward view of Maury Street crossing and Tower 207, with the Elysian Street Viaduct and Hardy Street Shops in the background. (Carl Codney Collection.)

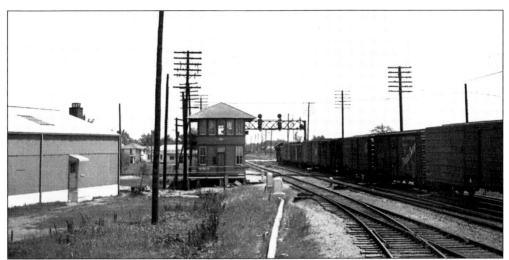

Tower 26 became operational on September 29, 1903, controlling the crossings of Southern Pacific's main line with the Gulf, Colorado & Santa Fe (later Houston Belt & Terminal) at Mary Street and with the Lufkin Subdivision in Houston's Fifth Ward. On June 21, 1907, the tower was moved east 750 feet and assumed control of Tower 25, which controlled the International–Great Northern crossing at Carr Street. Tower 26 assumed control of Tower 71 at Quitman Street on the Lufkin Subdivision on September 11, 1907. It became the busiest interlocking on SP in Texas, handling an average of 200 train and engine movements daily by 1946. In 1959, it assumed control of Tower 207 at Maury Street and the Centralized Traffic Control to Niles on the freight route. An interlocking designated as Tower 210, controlled from Tower 26 was established at the crossing of the Lufkin Subdivision and HB&T at Collingsworth Street. More territory was added when Tower 13 closed in 1966, adding Chaney Junction, Eureka, and Bellaire Junction. In the above photograph, an eastward train en route to Englewood passes Tower 26; below, the view faces west toward the tower with the HB&T in the foreground. (Joe R. Thompson courtesy of the Railroad and Heritage Museum, Temple, Texas.)

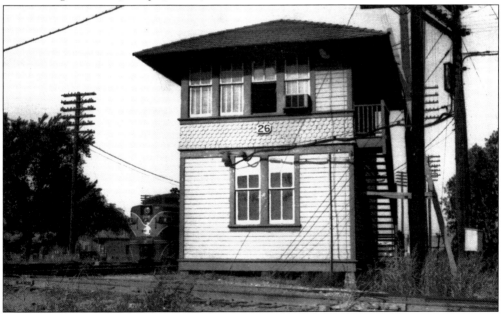

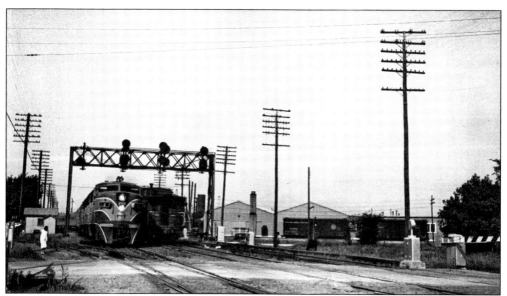

The eastbound Sunset Limited is meeting a westward freight train at West Road in the mid-1950s. The overhead signal bridge was located east of Tower 26, which is hidden behind the freight train. The track curving to the left at the crossing connects the SP to the Houston Belt & Terminal Railway, which crosses behind the signal bungalow. The Chicago Great Western boxcar in the background is on the HB&T. (Joe R. Thompson courtesy of Railroad and Heritage Museum, Temple, Texas.)

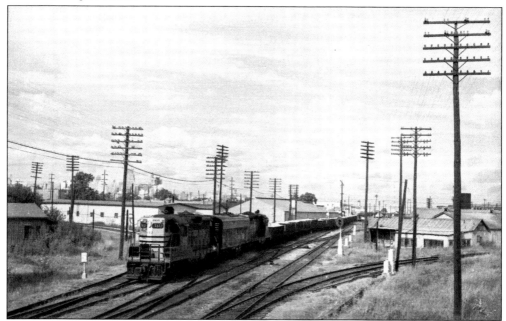

Above, a westbound loaded gravel train from Eagle Lake crosses the Lufkin Subdivision between Tower 26 and Maury Street in 1955. The track curving to the right is the connection to Lufkin and Shreveport. The connection curving to the left in front of GP9 No. 412 is the passenger route to Grand Central Station. The Lufkin Subdivision crossing is about 10 cars behind the locomotives. (Joe R. Thompson courtesy of the Railroad and Heritage Museum, Temple, Texas.)

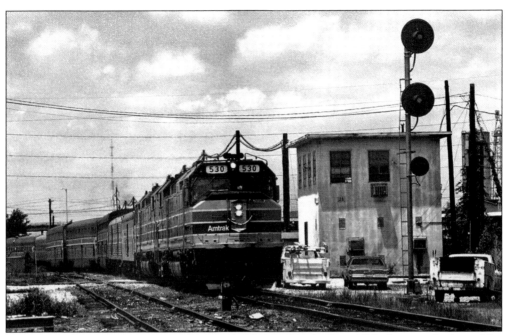

Amtrak's eastbound Sunset Limited is passing Tower 26 in the June 1978 photograph above. The tower was rebuilt in 1959, with a new steel structure was erected around the existing wooden building, which was removed from within as construction progressed. A new electric push button operated interlocking system was installed, replacing the obsolete 90-lever interlocking machine. Tower 26 was closed in 1988, and its functions were transferred to the Southern Pacific Rail Traffic Control (RTC) operator at Union Station. (Gary Morris.)

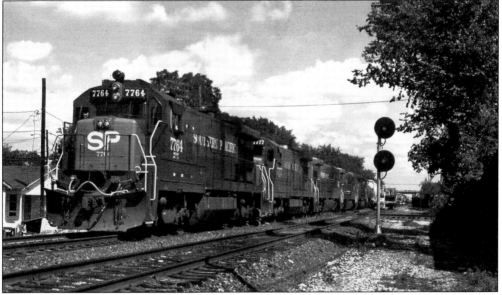

Train SRASK is approaching Tower 26 in Houston October 10, 1986, on its 876-mile trek from Strang to East St. Louis, Illinois. This train primarily handled petrochemicals from the Galveston line to connections with eastern railroads via the Alton & Southern Railroad at East St. Louis. At Tower 26, the train will head northward toward Shreveport. (Barry Byington Sr.)

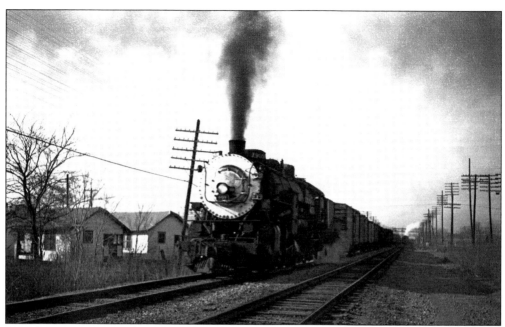

Joe Thompson captured two westbound trains on the double track between Tower 26 and Englewood Yard in 1950. Above, Extra 909 West thunders by houses in Houston's Fifth Ward. This locomotive, the third one to wear number 909, was nearing the end of its 30 years of service in 1953. Below, F3 diesel 300 leads an extra freight train. This was the busiest segment of track on Southern Pacific's lines in Texas. Originally constructed by the Texas & New Orleans Railroad in 1859, the line was double tracked in 1895, concurrent with the construction of Englewood Yard. (Joe R. Thompson courtesy of the Railroad and Heritage Museum, Temple, Texas.)

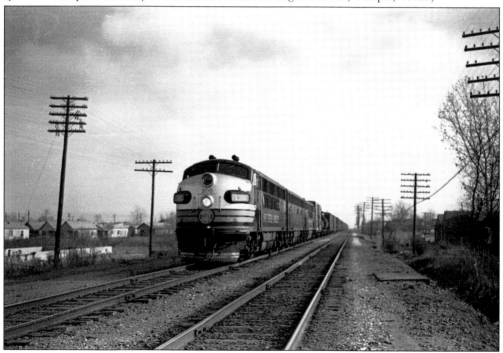

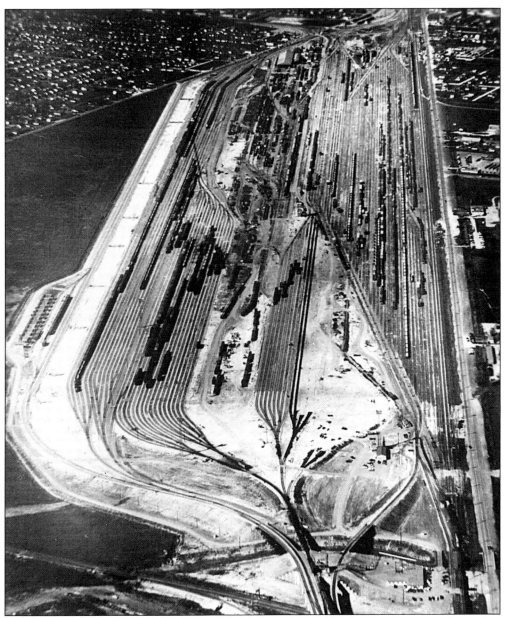

The Texas & New Orleans Railroad constructed Englewood Yard in 1895 in a rural area five miles west of downtown Houston. The first expansion of the yard was in 1913 to consolidate classification functions of three other yards at Englewood, relegating those yards to industry support. Operations from Hardy Street transferred to Englewood on November 15, 1914. Operations from Chaney Yard and from North Yard on the Lufkin Subdivision moved on February 15, 1915. In 1925, Englewood had 27 classification tracks and expanded to 36 tracks during World War II. By the 1950s, the flat-switched yard was inadequate to handle the approximately 3,500 cars switched daily, so plans were developed to build a larger and more efficient hump yard at a cost equivalent to $57 million in 2010. Construction of the new yard began in June 1953, and the initial 16 classification tracks were in service on December 20, 1954. Tracks from the original flat-switched yard are to the right in this 1954 image. (Southern Pacific.)

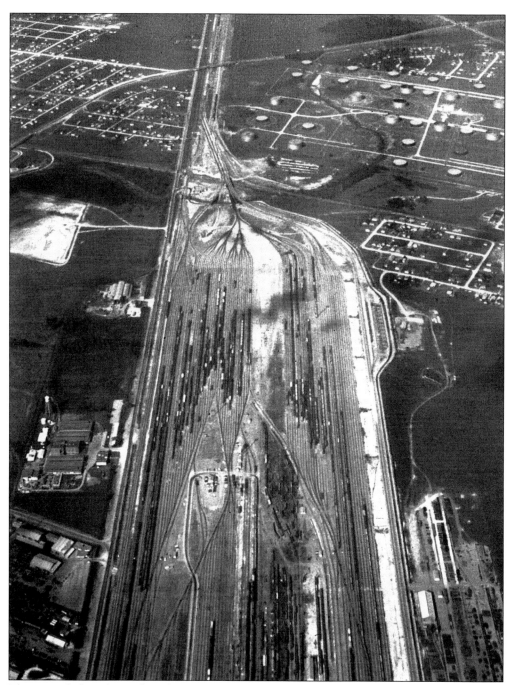

The expanded Englewood Yard was completed in 1956 and had 48 classification (bowl) tracks, 11 train departure tracks, 11 train arrival tracks, 10 local freight car tracks, three interchange tracks, and seven car repair tracks. The expanded yard had over 100 miles of track with a capacity of 6,000 freight cars. Sixteen additional classification (bowl) tracks were added in 1959. The original flat switched yard remained in service during the expansion of the yard and conversion to a gravity or "hump" yard. This aerial view was photographed in 1956 looking eastward. (Joe R. Thompson courtesy of the Railroad and Heritage Museum, Temple, Texas.)

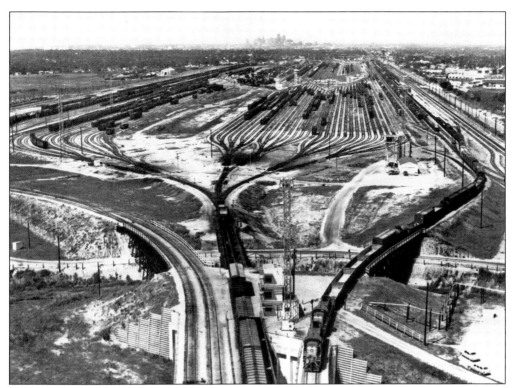

Cars are rolling down the hump into classification tracks in this westward view. The locomotives in the left-hand side are dragging cars to the hump, where they will be shoved over the 27-foot crest. Speed of the rolling cars is regulated automatically by retarders. At this time, there were 48 classification tracks; 16 additional tracks were added in 1959. (Southern Pacific courtesy of John Signor.)

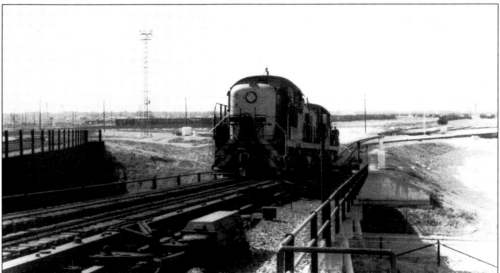

A pair of 1,600-horsepower RSD-5 locomotives are descending Englewood's hump in December 1956. One of the several sets of retarders used to regulate the speed of freight cars are visible in the foreground. (Joe R. Thompson courtesy of the Railroad and Heritage Museum, Temple, Texas.)

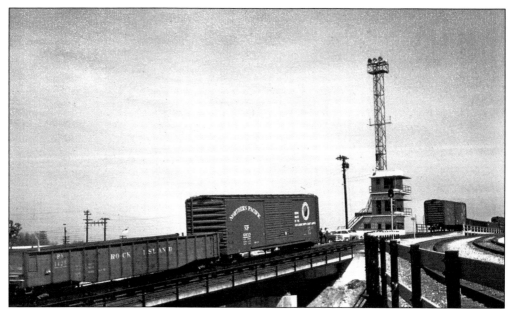

The top floor of the three-story Crest Tower at the crest of Englewood Yard hump was occupied by the yardmaster supervising crest operations. The second floor houses the yard conductor, who was in charge of the push button equipment controlling the power switches that route the cars into the proper classification track. On the first floor is the yard clerk who checks the switch lists and is in charge of the electronic scale weighing each car. (Joe R. Thompson courtesy of Railroad and Heritage Museum, Temple, Texas.)

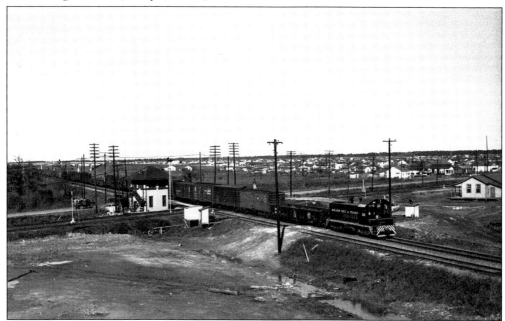

This eastward view from the crest in 1955 shows a Houston Belt & Terminal Railway train crossing the Southern Pacific main line at Tower 87. Liberty Road is visible to the left of the interlocking tower. Today the North Wayside Drive overpass occupied the land where the tower stood. (Dean Hale courtesy of the Railroad and Heritage Museum, Temple, Texas.)

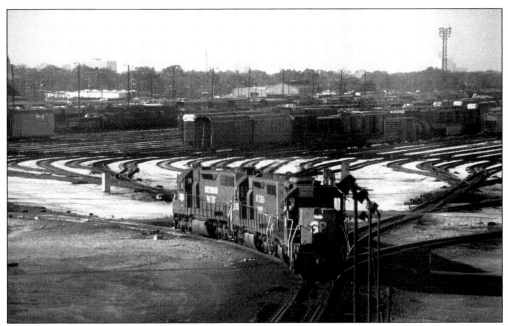

By the 1980s, the yard and Houston's skyline had undergone dramatic changes. After 23 years of service, the yard was in need of a major rehabilitation, which commenced in July 1979. The rails, ties, switches, retarders, and electronic scales from the crest to the two main switches where the two SD35R units are, above were replaced during a 24-hour shutdown of the hump on July 9. Beginning July 23 for seven days, 450 men worked around the clock to rehabilitate 32 bowl tracks, re-ballasting 18 miles of track with 600 carloads of ballast, replacing 29 switches and 25,000 ties. During 1980, the remaining 32 bowl tracks were rehabilitated, and in 1982, new retarders and a new computer system installed. (Steve Standifer.)

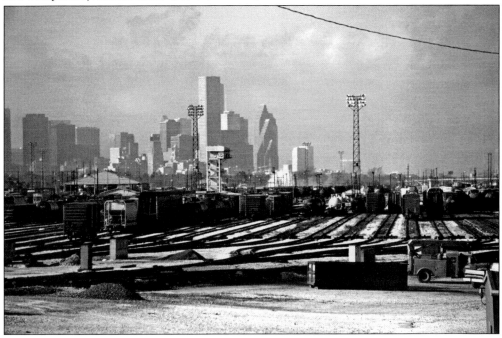

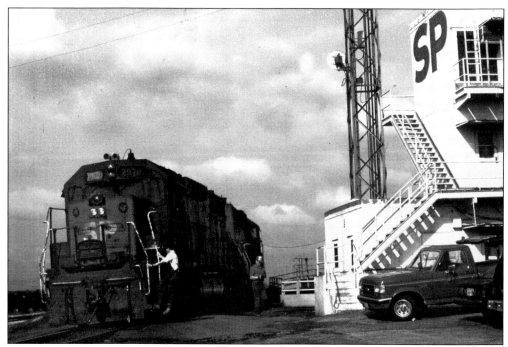

As a set of SD-35 hump engines pulls by the Crest Tower at Englewood Yard, one switchman has dropped off while another switchman boards the engine on April 16, 1991. The 2,000-horsepower SD-35s were used in two unit sets to push freight cars over the hump. (Tom Kline.)

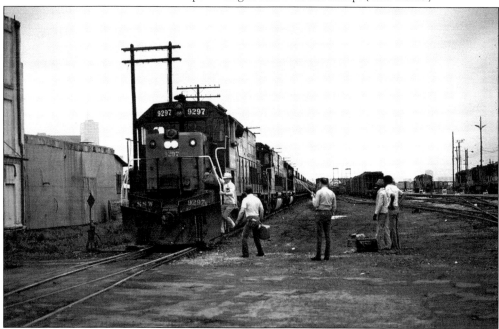

Under overcast skies on a gloomy April day in 1977, an eastward loaded unit sulphur train stops for a crew change at McKee Street, adjacent to Hardy Street Yard. This train originated at Newgulf, located 75 miles southwest of Houston, and is en route to Beaumont where it will be interchanged to the Kansas City Southern Railway. (Gary Morris.)

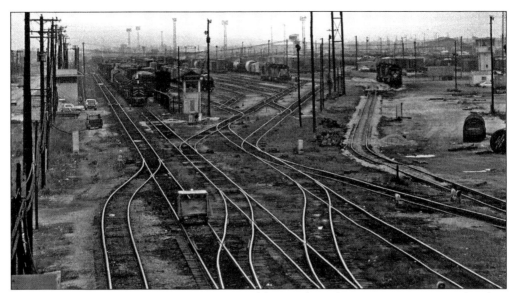

Above is the west end of Englewood Yard as viewed from Lockwood Drive overpass in 1981. The white building to the left of adjacent Liberty Road is Tower 68. On Main Track 1, a maintenance-of-way track car is moving eastward and, on Main Track 2, a train with two Missouri Pacific units is about to pass the west end switchman's shanty. (Gary Morris.)

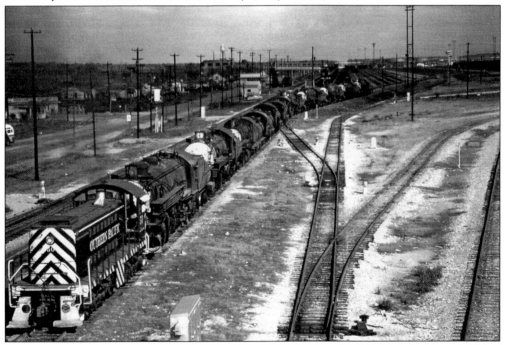

The Alco S2 switch engine No. 50 is moving 12 retired steam locomotives at the west end of Englewood Yard on January 8, 1957. These were the few remaining steam engines on the T&NO and were en route to Commercial Metals and Houston Compressed Steel for scrapping. In 1946, there were 649 steam engines assigned to Southern Pacific lines in Texas and Louisiana, reduced to 189 in 1953, to 80 in 1954, and 34 in 1955. Steam operations ended in 1957. (Joe R. Thompson courtesy of the Railroad and Heritage Museum, Temple, Texas.)

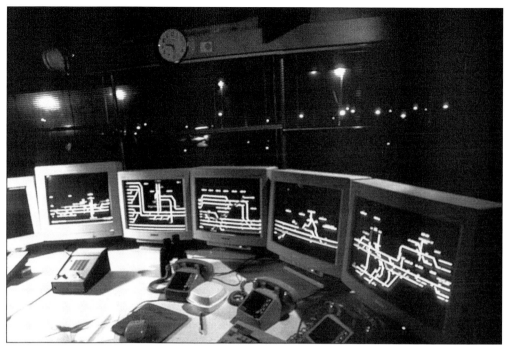

Tower 68 at the west end of Englewood Yard was placed in service in 1907. When these photographs were taken on September 8, 1996, the tower controlled from Tower 108 interlocking to Dawes, westward to but not including Chaney Junction and the Galveston line to Tower 86. The Digicon control system was the same used by the train dispatchers. The tower closed in 1999 when its functions were assumed by a Union Pacific (UP) train dispatcher in Spring, Texas. The building was razed in 2010. (Tom Kline.)

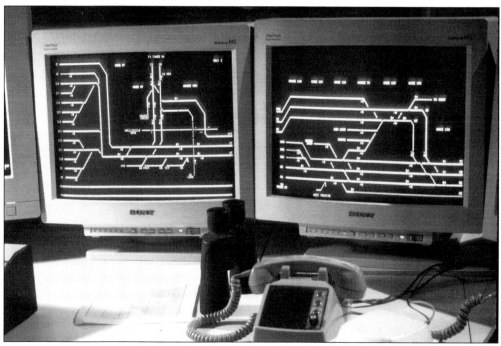

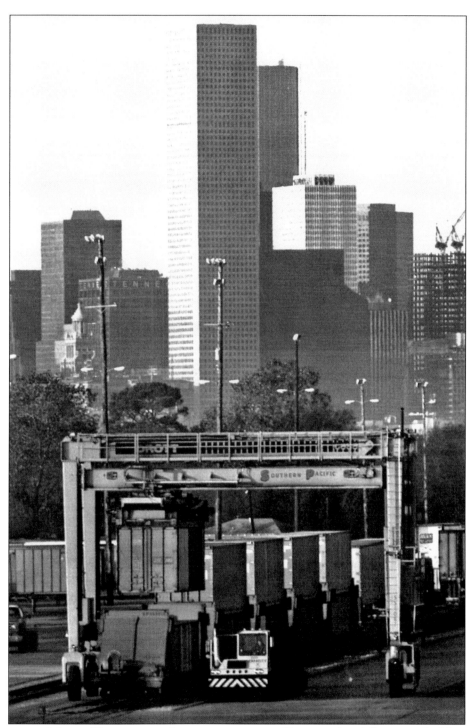
A giant mobile straddle crane is picking up a container off an articulated flat car at the Houston Intermodal Facility located at the western end of Englewood Yard. Southern Pacific began "piggyback" service in Texas transporting trailers on flat cars in 1953 from the Houston freight Station. (Southern Pacific.)

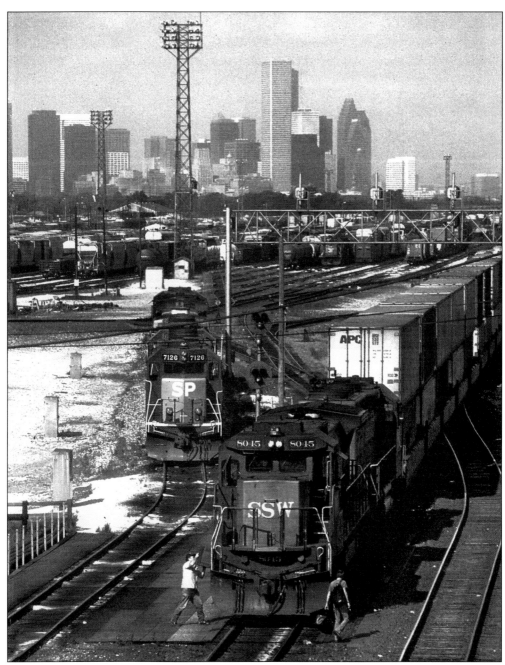

A New Orleans-bound double stack container train is changing crews near the east end of Englewood Yard. This crew will handle the train 210 miles to Lafayette, Louisiana, where another crew will take over for the remaining 135 miles to New Orleans. A crew change at Echo, Texas, 106 miles east of Englewood on the Sabine River, was eliminated in 1989. Southern Pacific pioneered the use of double stack container cars in 1979. Stacking containers permitted running shorter trains with heavier payloads, since a three-unit double stack car 171 feet long carries the same number of containers as six conventional flat cars with a length of 276 feet. (Southern Pacific courtesy of John Signor.)

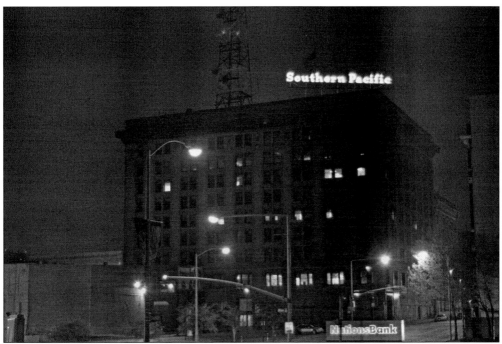

The Southern Pacific Building at 913 Franklin Avenue served as the regional headquarters for the Texas and Louisiana lines from 1910 until it was converted to condominiums in 1997. (Tom Kline.)

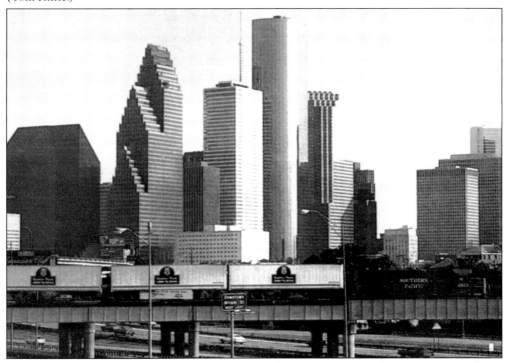

Train HODAQ (Houston to Dallas) is passing over the Interstate 45 viaduct in Houston. This is the same location as the bridge in the photographs on page 48. (Southern Pacific.)

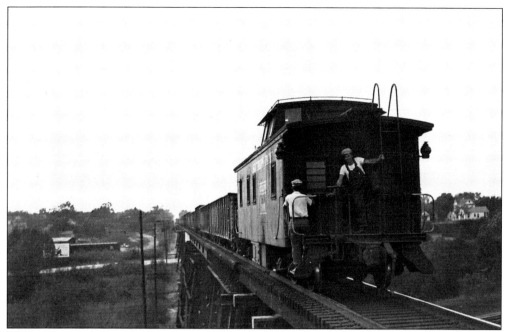

The conductor and rear brakeman on the caboose of an westward freight train enjoy the scenery as their train crosses the 429-foot-long viaduct over the Missouri–Kansas–Texas Railroad, White Oak Bayou, and U.S. Highway 75. Located about one half mile west of Hardy Street on the single track freight route, the wooden bridge was replaced by concrete ballast deck trestle in 1961 prior to construction of the Dallas Freeway, now Interstate 45. (Joe R. Thompson courtesy of the Railroad and Heritage Museum, Temple, Texas.)

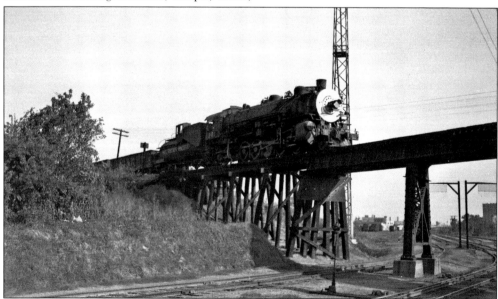

Extra 929 West is crossing over the Missouri–Kansas–Texas Railroad, also referred to as the Katy, at the east end of the viaduct in 1952. The large structure behind the locomotive is a light tower for Katy's City Yard nestled along the east bank of White Oak Bayou. (Joe R. Thompson courtesy of Railroad and Heritage Museum, Temple, Texas.)

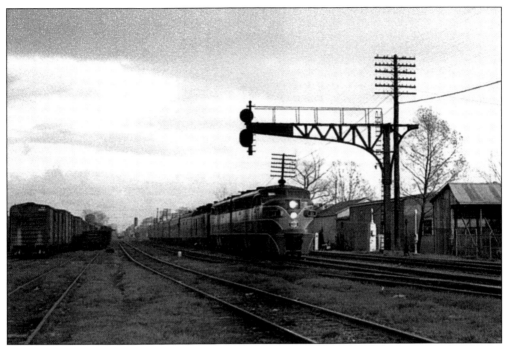

The Dallas-bound Sunbeam passes freight cars at Chaney Yard in Houston around 1954. Chaney Yard serviced industries between Houston and Eureka, as well as the 3.1-mile-long Heights Lead. (Dean Hale courtesy of the Railroad and Heritage Museum, Temple, Texas.)

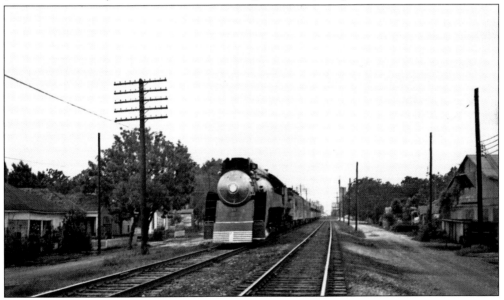

No. 14, the inbound Sunbeam from Dallas, passes through suburban Houston on the eastward main track between Eureka and Chaney Junction in 1953. The eastward main track was constructed by the Galveston & Red River Railway during 1853 and 1854. The westward main track was built by the Galveston, Harrisburg & San Antonio Railway in during 1917 and 1918, forming a double-track line between Houston and West Junction. (Joe R. Thompson courtesy of Railroad and Heritage Museum, Temple.)

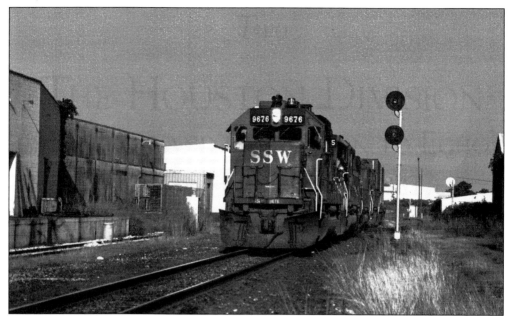

Niles was 1.6 miles west of Hardy Street on the single-track freight route. A 0.4-mile segment of two main tracks extended from Niles to the junction with the passenger route at Chaney Junction. In this photograph taken on August 8, 1993, the Train LBCXT (Long Beach, California, to CSX Railroad at New Orleans) is passing from two tracks to a single track at Niles. The train is carrying container traffic for Georgia and Florida. (David M. Bernstein.)

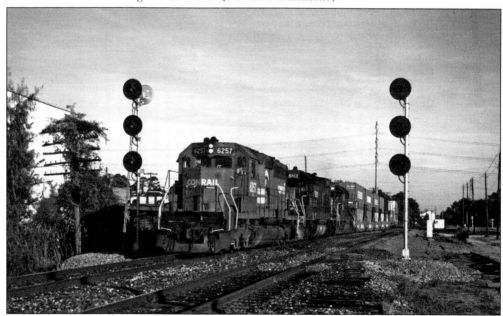

Passing the east limits of Eureka interlocking on a brilliant Sunday morning on August 15, 1993, is Train LBAVT (Long Beach, California, to Avondale, Louisiana). The white signal bungalow in the background marks the location where the Hearne Subdivision diverges from the double-tracked main line curving to the left. The train will be delivered to the Norfolk Southern Railroad in New Orleans. (David M. Bernstein.)

Two

THE HOUSTON DIVISION
HOUSTON AND GALVESTON TO ECHO
HOUSTON TO SHREVEPORT

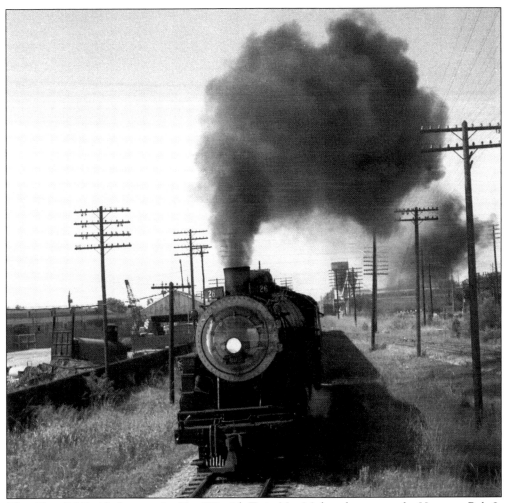

This Class P-9 Pacific locomotive No. 622 with Train No. 26 thunders across the Houston, Belt & Terminal Railway crossing at Interlocking 71 near Quitman Street on the Lufkin Subdivision. The train departed Houston's Grand Central Station at 9:10 a.m. and is two miles into its 232-mile run to Shreveport, Louisiana, where it is scheduled to arrive at 4:15 p.m. The photograph was taken in 1953. (Joe R. Thompson courtesy of the Railroad and Heritage Museum, Temple, Texas.)

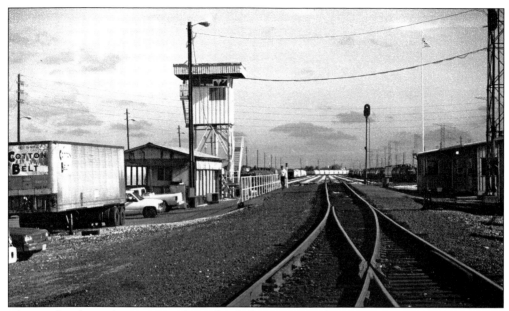

The rapid industrial expansion along the Galveston Line during the late 1970s necessitated construction of a hump yard at Strang, located 23 miles south of Houston. At this smaller version of Englewood Yard, cars were shoved over the hump and gravity rolled the cars to the classification tracks. The signal displays a green aspect, indicating to proceed shoving cars over the crest of the hump. (Tom Kline.)

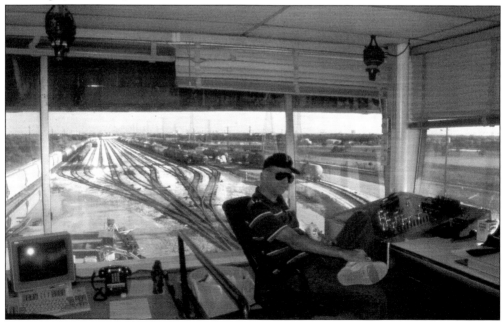

Yardmaster Mike Drumgould is manning the retarder control panel in the Strang Yard tower on July 11, 1993. Mike selects the classification track for each car shoved over the hump, and the computerized retarders control the cars speed. The 13-track hump yard at Strang opened in 1978, switching cars for the petrochemical plants and building trains for East St. Louis and New Orleans to bypass congested Englewood Yard in Houston. (Tim Kline.)

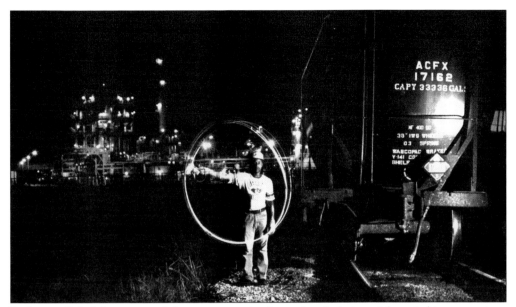

Brakeman B. L. Johnson signals his engineer using lamp signals during night switching operations at the Arco Chemical plant near Strang in 1981. The rapid industrial expansion between Houston and Texas City required 26 switch engines and trains per day by 1994. (Monte Bailey photograph courtesy of Southern Pacific.)

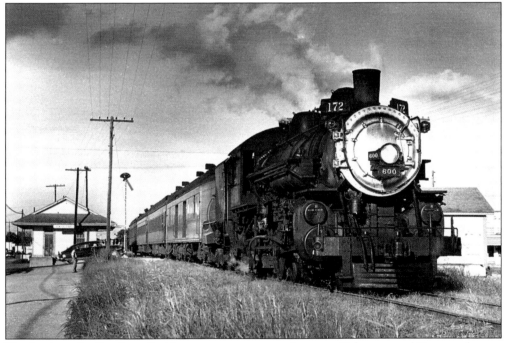

The final regular Southern Pacific passenger to operate between Galveston and Houston departs Pasadena on Saturday August 4, 1951. Trains 171 and 172 handled through sleeping cars between Dallas and Galveston until 1942 in connection with the Owl at Houston. In 1946, through sleeping car service between New Orleans and Galveston was established in connection with the Acadian at Houston. (Don Sims photograph courtesy of John Signor.)

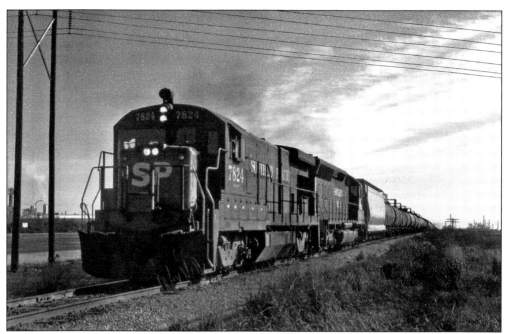

A westward trains passes through Deer Park en route to Strang on January 3, 1981. This is on the original line constructed during 1892 to 1894 by the La Porte, Houston & Northern Railroad. In 1961, SP abandoned 5.5 miles between Sinco Junction and Deer Park Junction (near the rear of this train), and the right-of-way was used to construct the Pasadena Freeway. A new line was constructed east of the original right-of-way, and a paired track operation was established with the Port Terminal Railroad Association. Centralized Traffic Control dispatched by Southern Pacific began on both lines. (David M. Bernstein Collection.)

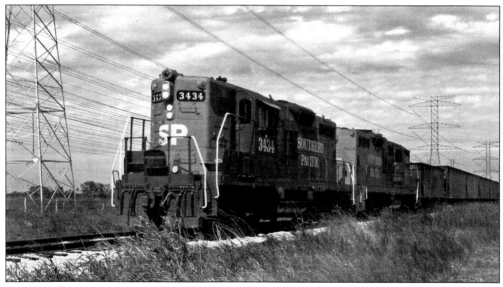

Two GP9 locomotives are leading a ballast train on the Galveston line near Kemah, 32 miles south of Houston, on October 19, 1980. This section of track was removed from service in 1988 when SP obtained trackage rights over the Galveston, Houston & Henderson Railroad. (David M. Bernstein.)

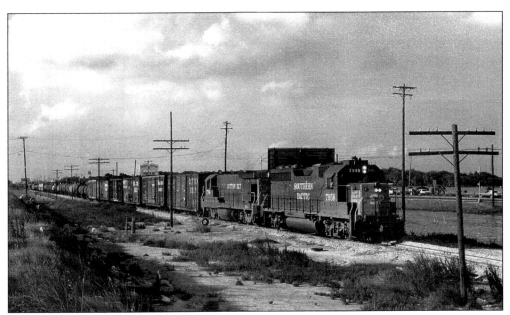

Train No. 221, the daily (except Saturday) local from Englewood to Galveston, is approaching the Clear Creek Draw Bridge at Seabrook on August 31, 1980. The two-color light signal in the bottom photograph is the interlocking signal for the drawbridge. The vehicular drawbridge in the background is Texas Highway 146. On September 25, 1988, the Galveston Subdivision was removed from service between milepost 29.3 near Joyce to milepost 41.1 near Nadeau. Effective the on same date, Southern Pacific trains serving Texas City and Galveston began operating over on the Galveston, Houston & Henderson Railroad (owned by the Missouri Pacific Railroad). The drawbridges over Clear Creek in Seabrook and over Dickinson Bayou in San Leon were permanently opened to water traffic. The out-of-service trackage remained in place until after being formally abandoned in 1996 (the abandonment was between mileposts 30.0 and 40.5). (David M. Bernstein Collection.)

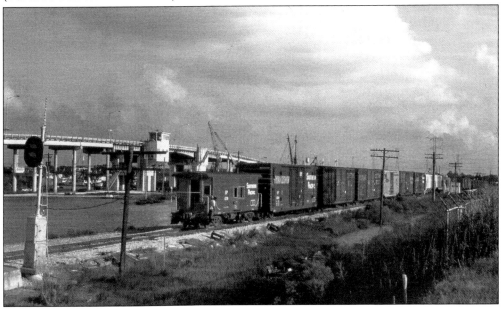

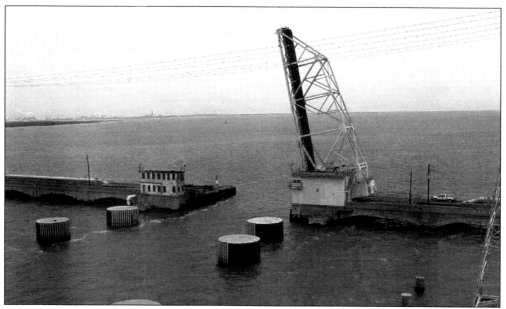

The two-mile-long Galveston Causeway was completed in 1911, replacing the wooden Santa Fe trestle used by four railroads to access Galveston since 1900, when the hurricane destroyed the other railroad bridges. Built at a cost equivalent to $33.1 million in 2010, the 28-arch bridge originally had two railroad tracks, one interurban railway track, and a roadway. The interlocking towers at Virginia Point and Island were closed in 1929 and their functions were transferred to the interlocking operator at the Lift Bridge. The original drawbridge was replaced in 1989. (David M. Bernstein Collection.)

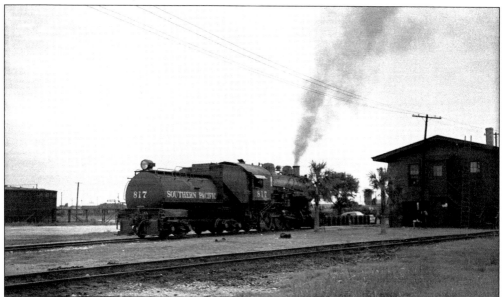

Engine 817 at the Galveston yard office in 1953. Southern Pacific owned wharves, piers, warehouses, oil storage facilities, a grain elevator, shops, and a roundhouse at Galveston. In 1955, Southern Pacific had 282,389 feet of yard, pier, and industrial tracks on Galveston Island. (Joe R. Thompson, courtesy of the Railroad and Heritage Museum, Temple, Texas.)

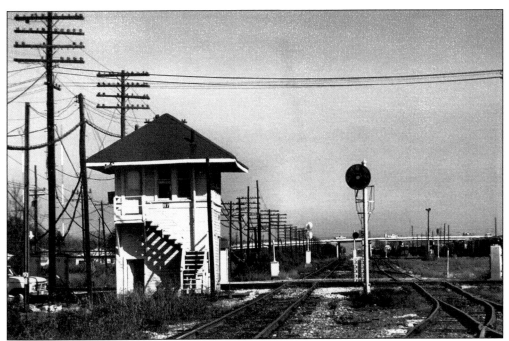

Above, a green signal beckons an eastward train at Tower 87 over the Houston Belt & Terminal crossing at the east end of Englewood in November 1977. Ahead lies 357 miles of single-track railroad to New Orleans. The interlocking tower was in service from February 13, 1911, until March 1, 1982, when its functions were assumed by the SP Rail Traffic Control operator at Union Station. The RTC position was abolished April 14, 1994, and Tower 68 at the west end of Englewood assumed control of the Tower 87 interlocking. Since the spring of 1999, the interlocking has been controlled by the Union Pacific train dispatcher. (Gary Morris.)

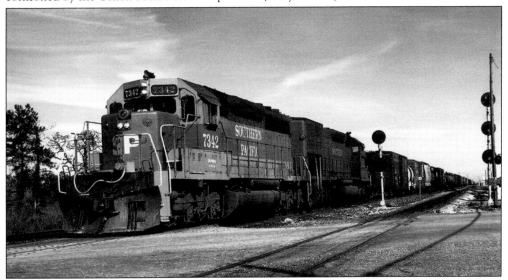

Painted in an experimental red and orange daylight paint scheme, SD40R No. 7342 leads a westward train over Mesa Road, two miles east of Tower 87, in December 1982. This location was the designated Mesa Crossover. No. 7342 was repainted in the traditional scarlet and gray colors in 1989. (Gary Morris.)

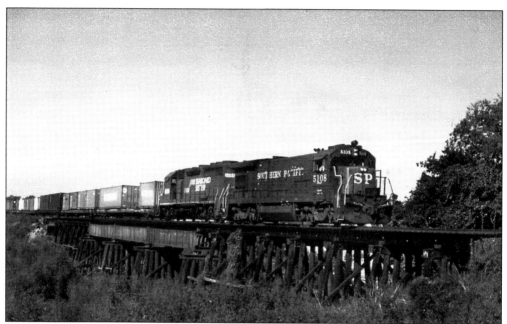

Train HOCXQ (Houston to New Orleans CSX Railroad) is crossing Greens Bayou, five miles east of Englewood, in October 1987. At the west end of the bridge is Dawes, where the double track through Houston begins. The second unit is a Seaboard System locomotive, which was a predecessor of CSX. After setting out cars at Avondale Yard, the train will be delivered to CSX Gentilly Yard in New Orleans. (Barry Byington Sr.)

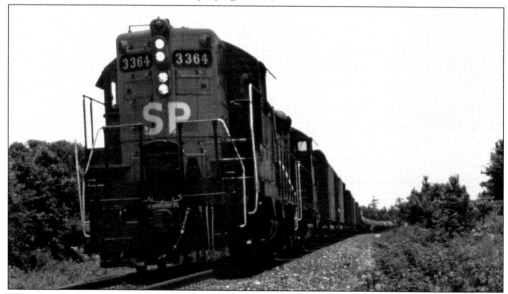

The westward Baytown Turn is approaching Sheldon, 10 miles from its terminus at Englewood Yard in Houston, on May 30, 1986. The train made a roundtrip between Englewood and Dayton, hauling primarily empty cars to the Baytown Branch Switchers and returning with primarily loaded cars. The Baytown Branch served U.S. Steel and major petrochemical producers including Exxon, Gulf Oil Company, J. M. Huber Company, Mobay Chemical Corporation, and Texas Eastern Corporation. (Tom Kline.)

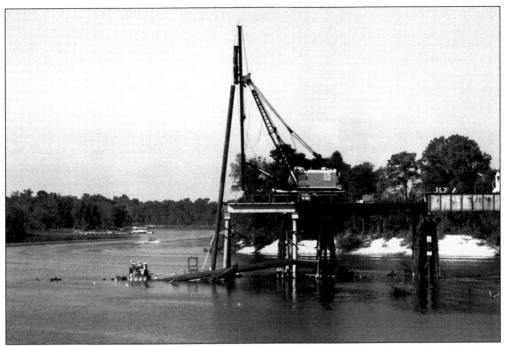

In October 1994, floodwaters washed away all of the five spans of the San Jacinto River Bridge at milepost 347 west of Sheldon. As a Southern Pacific bridge crew guides from below, a pile driver lifts a new pile into place during reconstruction of the bridge. (Tom Kline.)

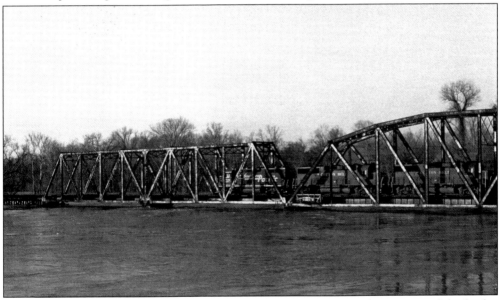

Train NOHOT (New Orleans to Houston) gingerly crosses the sinking spans of the bridge over the swollen Trinity River near Liberty on December 30, 1991. The western bridge pier was undermined by rapidly moving water that crested just 3 feet below the bridge deck. Concrete mixers were moved onto the bridge on flatcars, and cement was pumped to shore up the settling pier. SP stationed bridge crews to watch each train as it traversed the bridge at five miles per hour. Normally, the water level is 40 feet below the bridge at this location. (Tom Kline.)

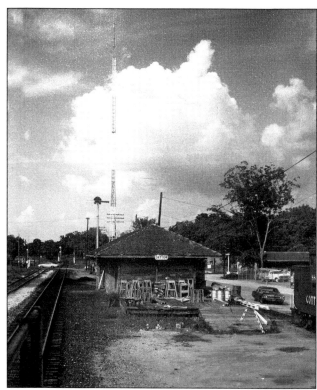

To the left is the station building at Dayton as viewed by an eastbound train in the 1980s. Dayton is located at the junction of the main line and the Baytown Branch 30 miles east of Englewood. The semaphore signal is a train order signal, one for each direction. When it is in the horizontal position, as shown in the photograph, a train must receive a clearance and train orders. When there are no orders to receive or the office is closed, the semaphore arms will be in a 45-degree down angle. These signals displayed red or green lights at night. (John Signor Collection.)

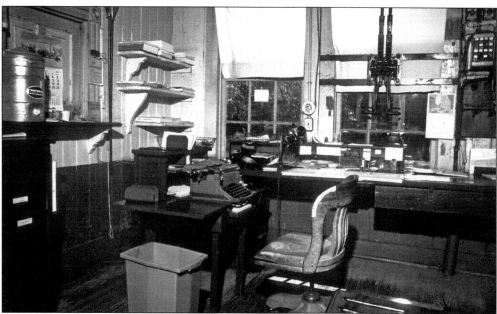

In this photograph is the interior of the Dayton station as it appeared in the 1980s. The mechanisms above the window controlled the train order signals. In 1931, the east siding switch was equipped with a power switch controlled from the station until Centralized Traffic Control was installed in 1982. The power switch enabled westward trains to enter the siding without stopping to line the switch on the one-percent grade. (John Signor Collection.)

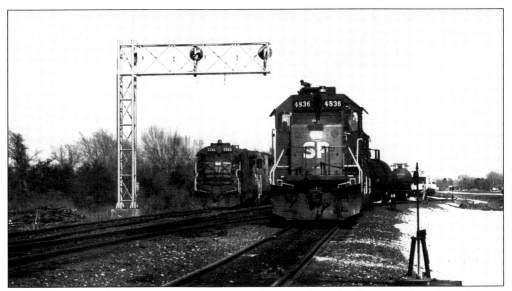

The Dayton Switcher using unit 4836 is switching cars from the Baytown Branch at the east end of Dayton yard on February 13, 1993. The westward Baytown Turn en route to Houston's Englewood Yard rests in the 13,000-foot-long passing siding. The intervening track is the Lafayette District main track between Houston and New Orleans. (Tom Kline.)

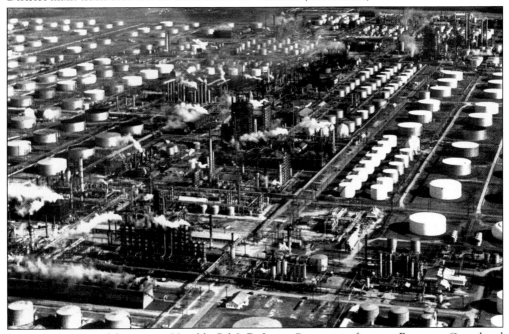

This aerial view is of the massive Humble Oil & Refining Company refinery at Baytown. Completed in 1919, the refinery was served from Houston via the Houston North Shore Railway and by the Dayton–Goose Creek Railway from Dayton. The Dayton–Goose Creek Railway (D-GC) constructed a 23-mile line from the SP at Dayton to Baytown in 1918 and a spur to Goose Creek in 1919. In 1923, Missouri Pacific subsidiary New Orleans, Texas & Mexico Railway was denied permission to acquire the D-GC by the Interstate Commerce Commission. Southern Pacific acquired control of the Dayton–Goose Creek Railway in 1926. (John Signor Collection.)

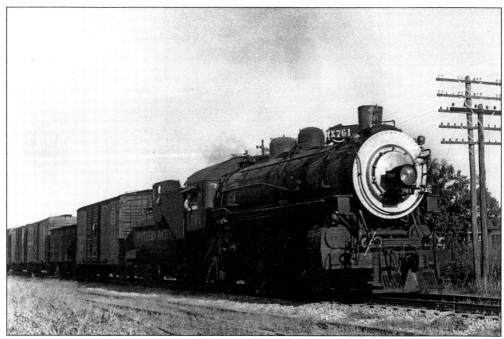

Extra 761 East rolls through Liberty, 37 miles east of Englewood Yard, on September 3, 1955, during the waning days of steam power. No. 761 was one of the last handful 2-8-2 Mikado Type locomotives in use at that time and the last one to be scrapped, on September 14, 1956, in Houston. By the end of 1955, there were about 30 operating steam locomotives on Southern Pacific's lines in Texas and Louisiana. Note the head brakeman is riding in the "doghouse" on top of No. 861's tender. (Verner Barber photography courtesy of Steele Craver.)

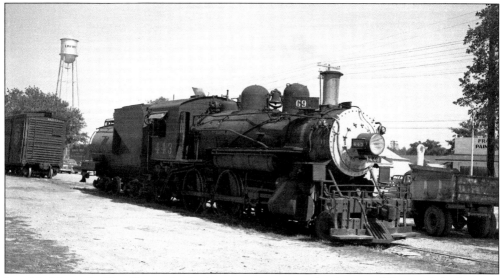

Local freight train No. 69 rests in the house track next to the depot at Liberty while the crew eats lunch. This local operated on Tuesday, Thursday, and Saturday between Beaumont and Houston's Englewood Yard. Locomotive 2-6-0 Mogul Type locomotive No. 443, built in 1899, was nearing its September 30, 1953, date with the scrapper. (Joe R. Thompson courtesy Railroad and Heritage Museum, Temple, Texas.)

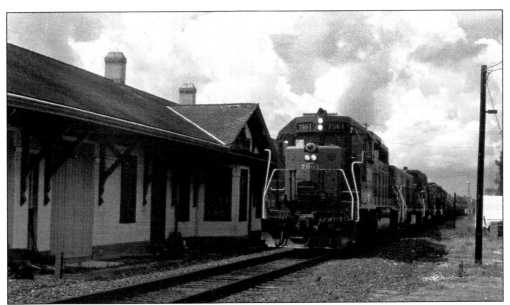

Train HONOM (Houston to New Orleans) is rolling by the depot at Liberty at 12:23 p.m. on September 26, 1986. Below, at 1:05 p.m. on the same day, the train is waiting in the 11,700-foot-long siding at Devers to let Amtrak's eastbound Sunset Limited by. The HONOM operated from Houston's Engelwood Yard to the Seaboard System (later CSX) at Gentilly Yard in New Orleans, 361 miles on a 30-hour schedule. The locomotive consisted of three 7960 series 3,000-horsepower GP40R "mother" units mated with two cabless 1600 series slug units. Designated as tractive effort booster units (TEBU), the slugs were rebuilt from U25B locomotives at Southern Pacific's shops in Sacramento, California. They were fitted with dynamic braking and fuel tanks with pumps to deliver diesel fuel to the mother units, but produced no horsepower. (David M. Bernstein.)

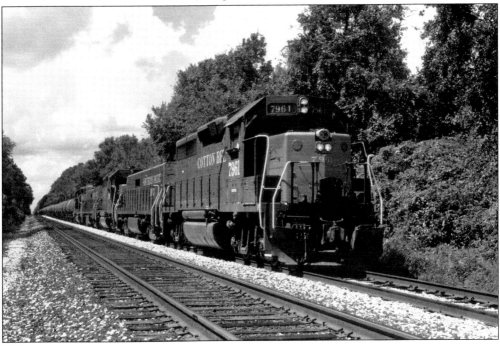

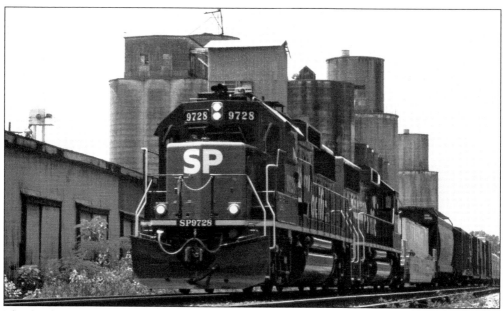

The Quality Special is heading eastward past the large concrete rice elevators at Devers on April 2, 1992. Originally dubbed "The New SP Train", it made a 20-city tour along Southern Pacific lines between March 23 and May 22, consisting of two locomotives and seven freight cars. At each stop, customers viewed the equipment and were given a presentation about the railroad's positive changes underway and future plans. Approximately 1,200 customers participated. (Tom Kline.)

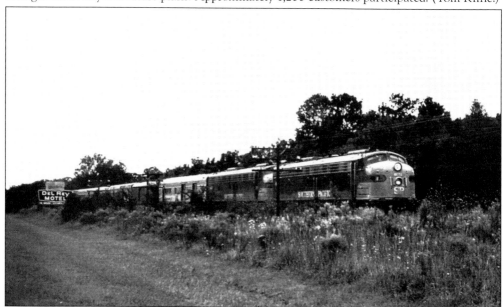

According to the sign advertising the Del Ray Motel along U.S. Highway 90, the eastbound Sunset Limited is between Devers and Ames on October 11, 1965. The number "2" in the train indicator on the locomotive identifies this as Train No. 2. By 1964, all trains displayed engine numbers in the indicators except Trains 1 and 2, and in 1967 the use of train indicators was discontinued. The motel no longer exists. (Joe R. Thompson courtesy of the Railroad and Heritage Museum, Temple, Texas.)

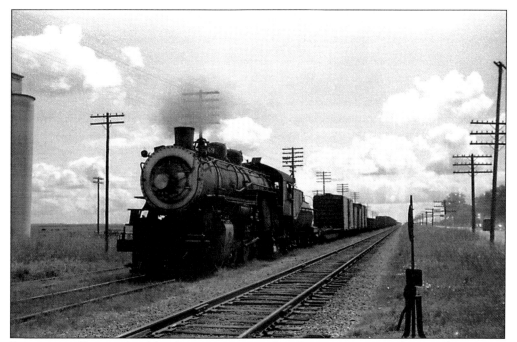

Beaumont to Houston local freight No. 69 waits in the siding at Nome, 18 miles east of Beaumont, in this 1954 photograph. Based on Houston Division Timetable No. 43, it is likely No. 69 was here to meet No. 6, the Argonaut, due at 9:20 a.m., and No. 2, the Sunset Limited, due at 9:38 a.m. There was an eight-mile branch line extending north from Nome to Sour Lake that was abandoned in 1933. (Joe R. Thompson courtesy of the Railroad and Heritage Museum, Temple, Texas.)

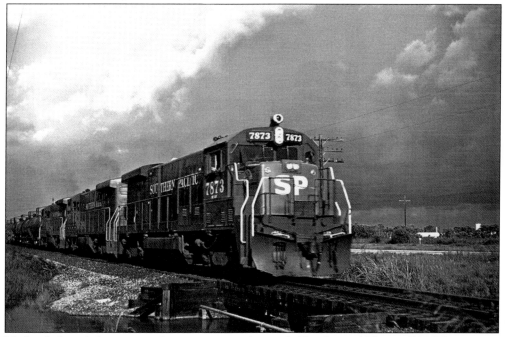

Under dark and threatening skies, an eastward train led by General Electric B30-7 locomotive 7873 rolls through China, 13 miles west of Beaumont, in September 1980. (Paul Sartori.)

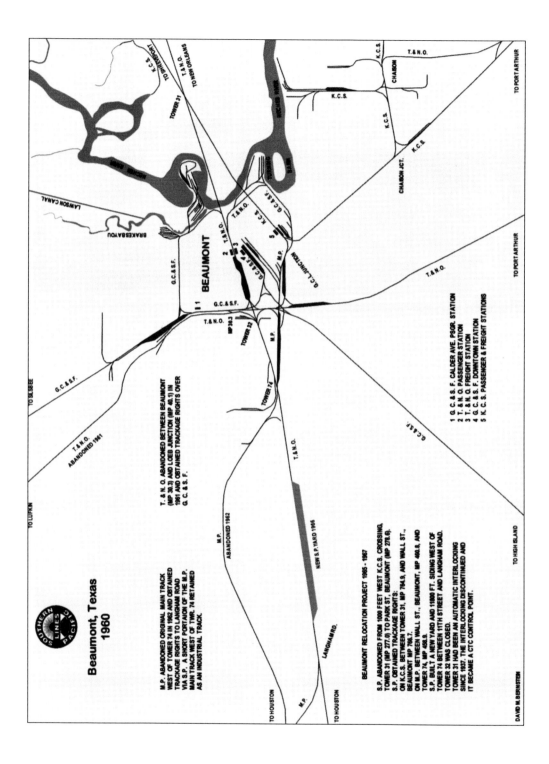

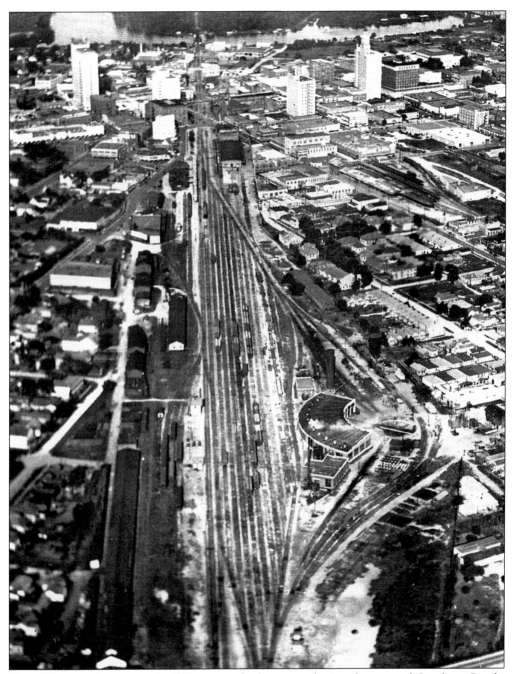

This 1950s aerial photograph of Beaumont looking east depicts the original Southern Pacific facilities before the 1967 relocation project. To the west just out of the photograph are the crossings of the SP mainline with the Sabine and Rockland Branches and the crossing of the Gulf, Colorado & Santa Fe Railway at Tower 32. At the top (east) end of the yard to the left of the main track is the passenger station, and to the right is the freight station. The Neches River is visible at the top of the photograph. (John Signor Collection.)

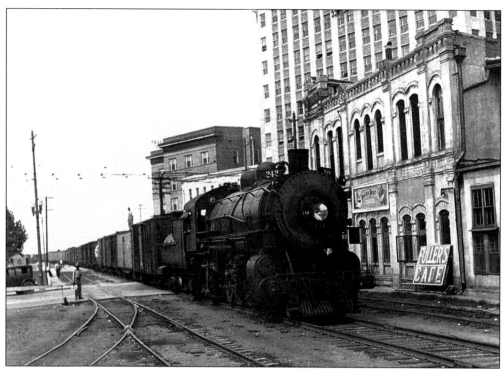

New Orleans-bound Train No. 242 is passing Fuller's Cafe in downtown Beaumont. Note the brakeman riding the top of the second car in the train, a practice outlawed today. (Harold K. Vollrath.)

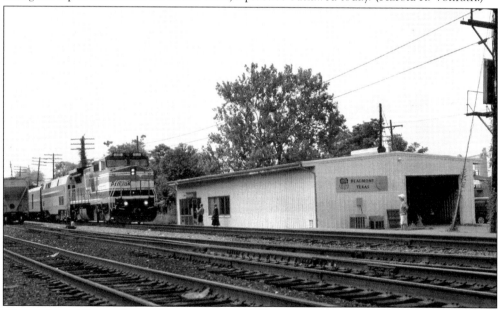

The eastbound Sunset Limited is stopping at the Beaumont passenger station on September 4, 1994. The station also housed the interlocking operators who moved from Tower 74, which was closed in July 1967. The tower was located about 500 feet east of here, where the Missouri Pacific crossed prior to the 1967 relocation project. The station building was closed in 2000 and razed a few years later. Amtrak trains still stop at a platform where the station once stood. (Jimmy Barlow.)

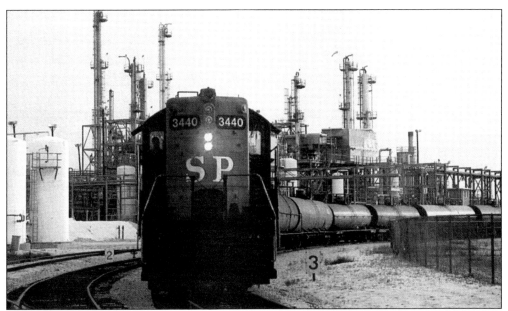

Southern Pacific switch engine is at work in the Pennwalt Corporation chemical plant near the Port of Beaumont in 1979. Driven by the increase in petrochemical traffic in the Beaumont/Orange/Port Arthur area, SP converted the Beaumont yard to a hump yard in 1979. (Southern Pacific.)

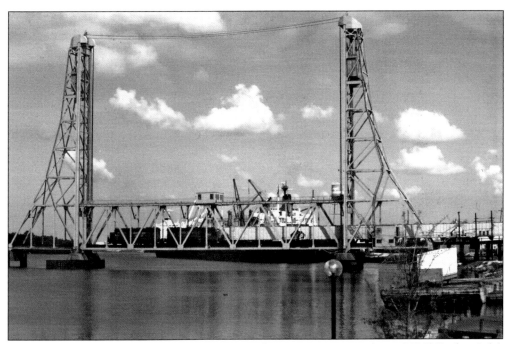

An eastward Southern Pacific train is crossing the Kansas City Southern (KCS) Railway's lift bridge over the Neches River at Beaumont on July 2, 1987. Southern Pacific abandoned two miles of its main line through downtown Beaumont between Park Street and 1,000 feet west of the KCS crossing on the east side of the river during the 1967 relocation. (Jimmy Barlow.)

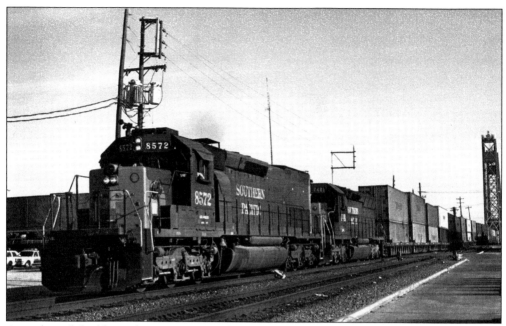

A westbound double stack container train has just crossed Pearl Street in downtown Beaumont in December 1987. Following the 1967 relocation project, Southern Pacific trains operated on the Kansas City Southern Railway for 1.8 miles from Tower 31 on the east side of the Neches River to College Street, then over the Missouri Pacific Railroad (MP) for 0.8 mile from College Street to the Tower 74 interlocking. The MP abandoned the line from Tower 74 west to Langham Road in 1962 and began operating over on the SP line. (Paul Sartori.)

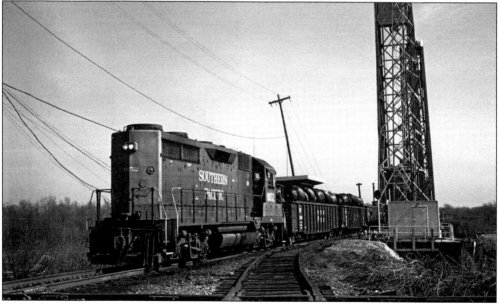

This westward Southern Pacific train is on the Kansas City Southern Railway crossing the Neches River at Beaumont in March 1989. The track crossing the KCS in the foreground serves the Port of Beaumont. The SP bridge crossing the Neches River was one-half mile north of here and was abandoned during the 1967 railroad relocation project. (Paul Sartori.)

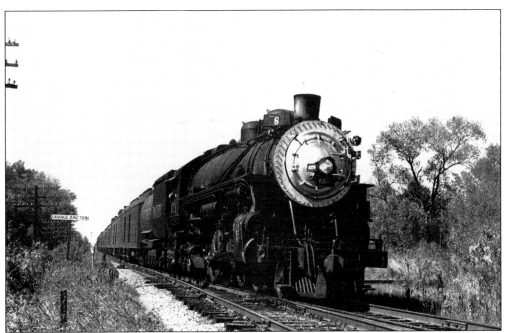

Class P-9 Pacific Type locomotive No. 626 leads Train No. 8, the eastbound Alamo, at Orange Junction in 1950. The main track curves to the right and the straight track is the Front Street track leading to the freight depot, industries, and wharves. In 1950, the Alamo operated between San Antonio and New Orleans, carrying sleeping cars between San Antonio and Houston, a newsagent lunch car between Houston and New Orleans, and coaches. Trains 7 and 8 were discontinued between San Antonio and Houston in 1951 and Houston and New Orleans in 1952. (Roger S. Plummer courtesy of Gordon Bassett.)

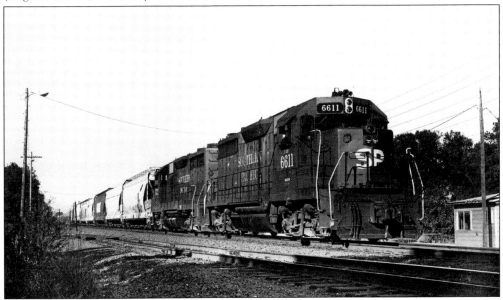

An eastbound local is stopped at West Orange on November 6, 1987, six miles from the Louisiana border at Echo. Orange, located one mile east, was the last passenger stop in Texas, 927 miles east of El Paso. (Jim Shaw.)

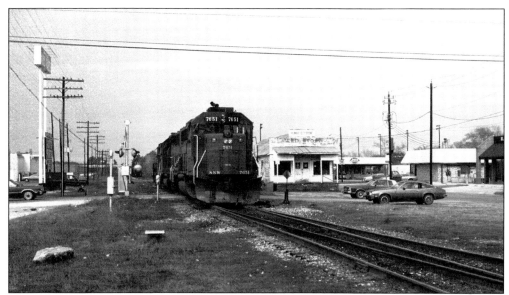

A westward train en route to Houston has cut the locomotives off and is proceeding over Higgins Street at Humble to enter the siding on February 10, 1980. They were giving their third locomotive to an eastward train that was on the main track behind the photographer. The east siding switch has since been moved 0.3 mile west, clear of Main Street. (George W. Hamlin.)

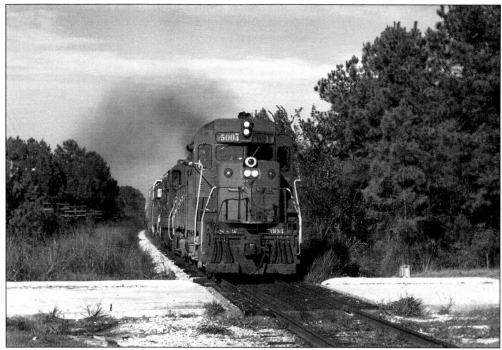

Cotton Belt GP30 No. 5007 leads a westward freight train into Humble on January 16, 1979. Humble, located 15 miles geographically north (railroad east) of Tower 26 was the first train order office and first siding on the Lufkin Subdivision. The siding was 9,147 feet long at the time, and often trains were held there until Engelwood Yard was ready to take them. The siding has since been shortened to 8,900 feet in length. (George W. Hamlin.)

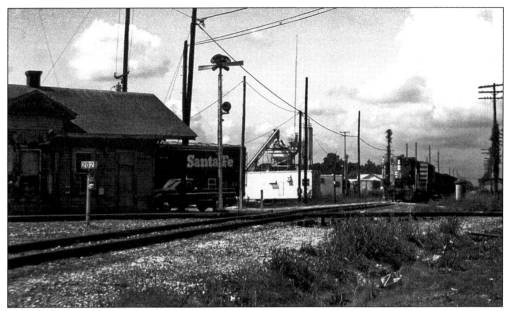

The westbound Cleveland Turn from Englewood Yard is switching cars at Cleveland in June 1980. Cleveland, located 44 miles from Tower 26, had a joint Southern Pacific/Santa Fe station and was an interchange point between the two railroads. The railroad crossing at grade was protected by stop signs until 1954, when an automatic interlocking was installed (Tower 202). (Joe R. Thompson courtesy of the Railroad and Heritage Museum, Temple, Texas.)

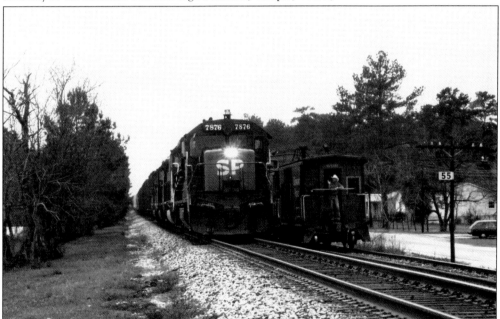

Crewmembers exchange greetings at a meet in Shepherd on March 17, 1989. Locomotive 7876 leads an eastward train en route to Lufkin on the main track, passing the caboose of the westward train in the siding. Mileposts on the Lufkin Subdivision were numbered from zero at Semmes Junction in Houston to 230.8 at Jordan Street in Shreveport. Timetable direction from Houston to Shreveport was eastward, and from Shreveport to Houston was westward. (Tom Kline.)

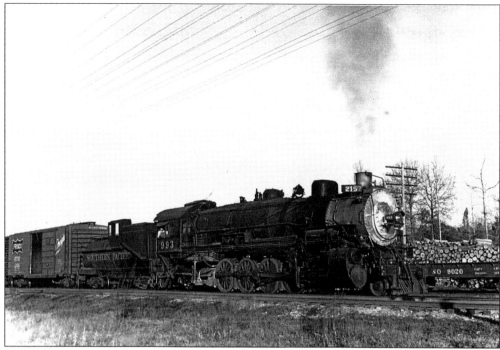

F-1 Class 2-10-2 No. 993 leads Train No. 215 at Midline, milepost 36, on February 3, 1954. No. 215 was the local freight train from Houston's Englewood Yard to Lufkin. No. 993 is working out its last few months of service before being scrapped on June 25, 1954. (Verner Barber photograph courtesy of Steele Craver.)

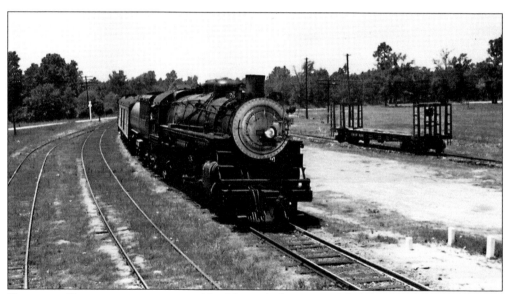

Houston to Shreveport passenger train No. 26 rounds the curve at Moscow, 88 miles from Houston, in a photograph taken around 1953. The tracks, from left to right, are the storage track, the siding, the main track, and the house track, which has a flat car for log loading. (Joe R. Thompson courtesy of the Railroad and Heritage Museum, Temple, Texas.)

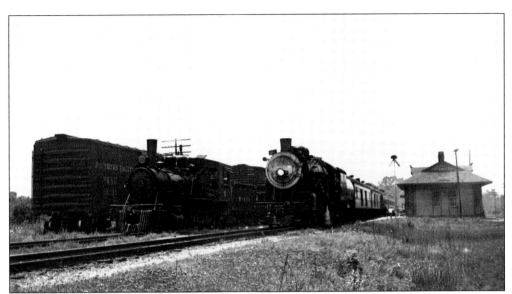

Moscow, Texas, located on the Lufkin Subdivision 88 miles north of Houston, was the interchange location between Southern Pacific and the 7-mile Moscow, Camden & San Augustine Railroad (MC&SA). The MC&SA was constructed to handle traffic for the W. T. Carter and Brother Lumber Company in Camden. On May 22, 1952, MC&SA Mixed Train No. 1 from Camden is interchanging passengers with SP Houston to Shreveport, Louisiana, Train No. 26. (Joe R. Thompson courtesy of Railroad and Heritage Museum Temple.)

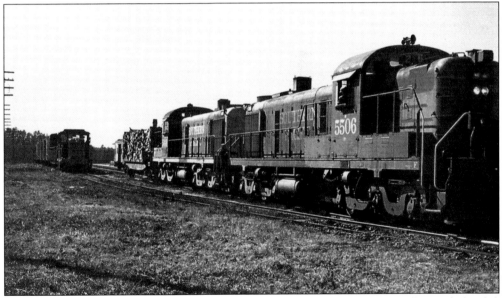

Thirteen years later Moscow, Camden & San Augustine Train No. 1 (now handling only freight) is swapping cars with Southern Pacific Train No. 216, the "Rabbit Local" between Houston and Lufkin. Although SP had discontinued passenger service here in 1955, the MC&SA continued handling passengers until July 1973. They did not purchase a diesel locomotive until 1961 and continued operating steam engines until January 1965, making the MC&SA the last non-tourist railroad in Texas regularly operating steam locomotives. (Joe R. Thompson courtesy of the Railroad and Heritage Museum Temple, Texas.)

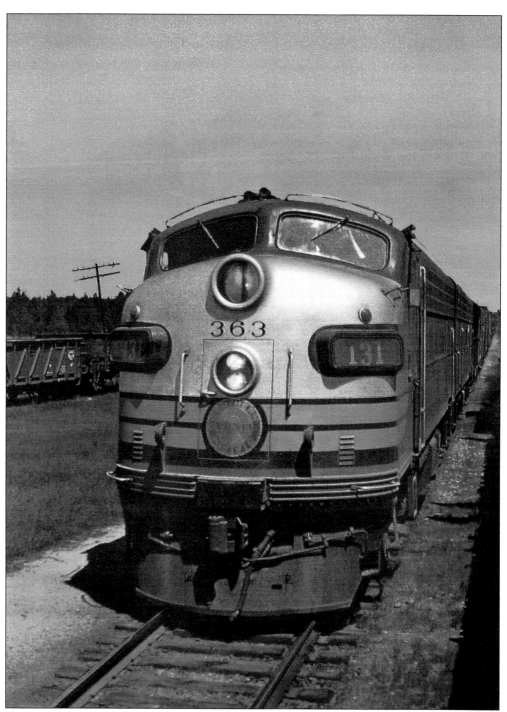

Viewed from Moscow, Camden & San Augustine Railroad's mixed train, Southern Pacific freight train No. 131 rolls through Moscow on April 6, 1957. No. 131 operated from daily from Shreveport to Englewood Yard in Houston, connecting with the Cotton Belt at Shreveport. Diesel No. 363 is a 1,500-horsepower model F7A built by the Electo-Motive Division of General Motors in 1953. (Joe R. Thompson courtesy of the Railroad and Heritage Museum, Temple, Texas.)

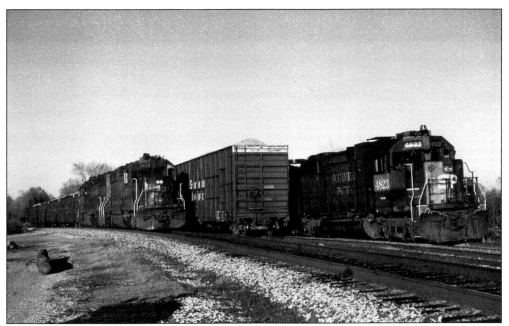

The "Termite Train" hauling wood chips to the Port Terminal Railroad Association in Houston is stopped on the main track at Moscow on January 4, 1996. The Corrigan Switcher with engine 4923 is switching the Moscow, Camden & San Augustine Railroad interchange cars in the yard. The freight car between on the track between the trains is a high-side open-top gondola car used to transport wood chips. (Tom Kline.)

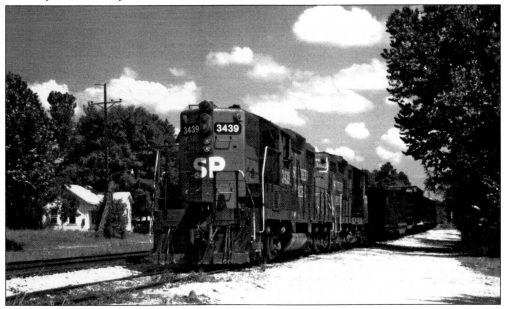

Two GP9 locomotives assigned to the Corrigan Switcher idle in the siding at Corrigan, milepost 93, on August 25, 1981 while the crew takes their lunch break. The switcher originated at Corrigan and worked the stations Lufkin, Diboll, Corrigan, Moscow, New Willard, Leggett, and Livingston. This job also handled the interchange with the Texas South–Eastern Railroad at Diboll. (John Carr.)

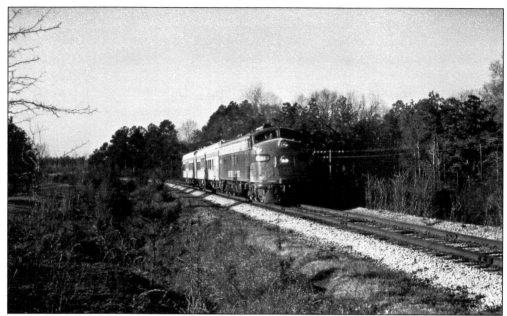

A special passenger train from Houston to Shreveport carrying Southern Pacific Company president Benjamin F. Biaggini and other company officials rolls through the East Texas piney woods between Corrigan and Diboll on January 28, 1965. The train consists of 2,400-horsepower E9A locomotive 6053 and Southern Pacific business cars No. 107, the Del Monte, and No. 140, the Stanford. (Joe R. Thompson courtesy of the Railroad and Heritage Museum, Temple, Texas.)

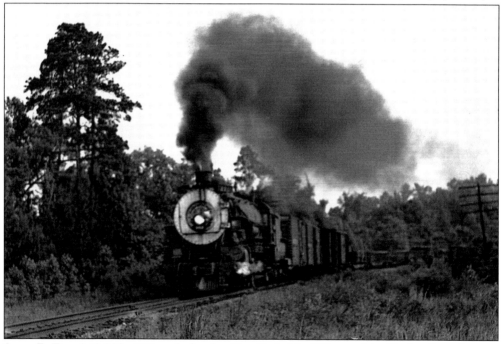

Santa Fe Type 2-10-2 No. 964 works hard pulling Train No. 215 out of the Neches River bottom near Diboll on May 8, 1954. The local freight train from Houston is about 13 miles from its terminus at Lufkin. (Joe R. Thompson courtesy of the Railroad and Heritage Museum, Temple, Texas.)

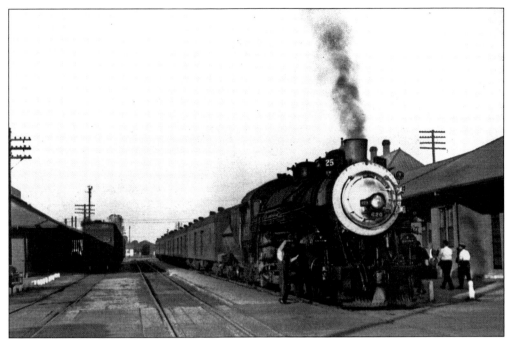

The fireman is performing his oiling duties on the handsome Pacific Type locomotive No. 620 at Lufkin. Train No. 25 is halfway on its 232-mile run from Shreveport to Houston. (Joe R. Thompson courtesy of the Railroad and Heritage Museum, Temple, Texas.)

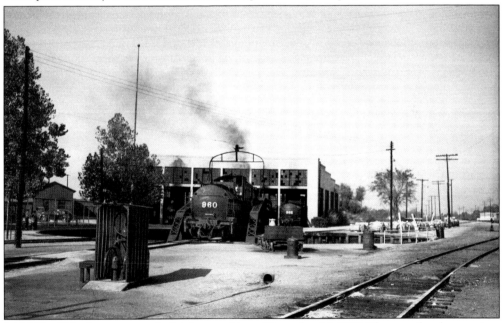

2-10-2 No. 980 takes a turn on Lufkin's turntable on November 15, 1950. There are four locomotives occupying the seven-stall roundhouse. Lufkin was the crew change point between Houston and Shreveport. In the mid-1950s, the roundhouse serviced locomotives for four local freight trains: No. 215 from Houston, No. 216 to Houston, No. 217 to Shreveport, and No. 218 from Shreveport. (Joe R. Thompson courtesy of the Railroad and Heritage Museum, Temple, Texas.)

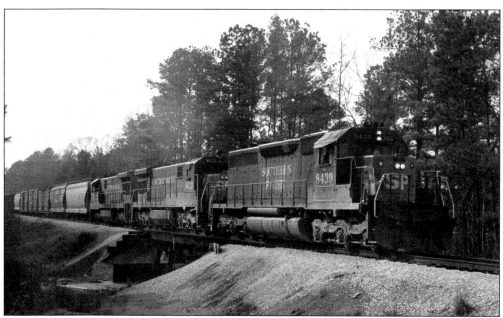

The Rockland Subdivision was a 172-mile line between Beaumont and Jacksonville, part of a through route to Dallas bypassing Houston. The Rockland Subdivision trains used the Shreveport Subdivision for 4.6 miles through Nacogdoches between Dorr Junction and Bonita Junction. In 1957, Southern Pacific abandoned 17 miles through the Angelina River bottoms between Dunagan and Nacogdoches. Trackage rights were obtained over the Angelina & Neches River Railroad from Dunagan to a connection with the Shreveport Subdivision at Prosser on the north side of Lufkin. During 1972 and 1973, the branch was upgraded to handle heavy chemical trains. In the photograph above, train BTASM (Beaumont to East St. Louis) is making the maximum 30-miles-per-hour speed at Doucette, 57 miles north of Beaumont, on December 27, 1979. Below, the BTASM is leaving the Angelina & Neches River Railroad and entering the Shreveport Subdivision at Prosser on August 30, 1985, one year before through service via the Rockland Branch ceased. (Jimmy Barlow.)

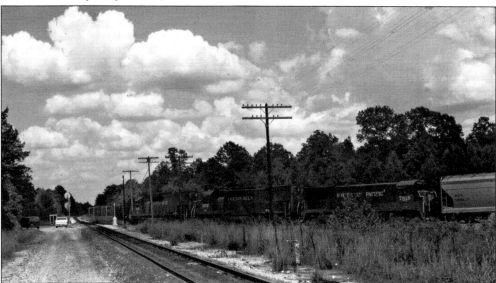

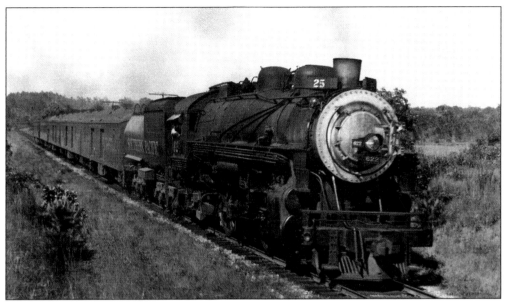

Train No. 25 is approaching Nacogdoches on one of its final runs in the summer of 1954. The Shreveport to Houston daylight train and its counterpart No. 26 were discontinued in Texas on August 4, 1954. A train with a single coach was operated between Shreveport and Logansport until August 9, since the authority for discontinuance in Louisiana was effective on that date. Night trains 27 and 28 were discontinued September 29, 1955, ending SP passenger service between Houston and Shreveport. (Harold K. Vollrath.)

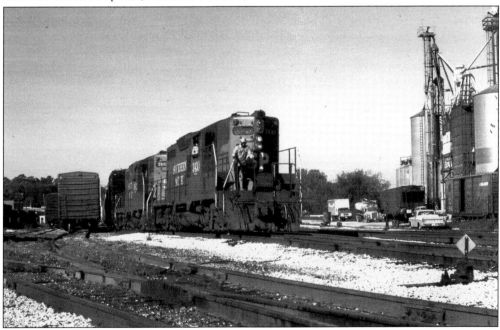

The Nacogdoches Switcher is working in the yard with two GP9 locomotives and a smiling crew on a cold November afternoon in 1981. The switcher worked the main line, the remainder of the old line to Dunagan and the Jacksonville Branch. Holly Farm Products, International Paper, Lone Star Fertilizer, Ready Mix Concrete, and other customers kept the switcher busy. (Tom Kline.)

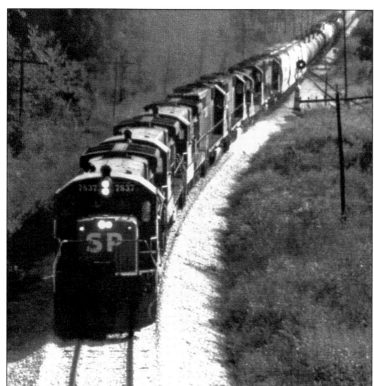

Eight locomotives power a westward train en route to Shreveport up the 1.2-percent grade through Bonita Junction in September 1981. Bonita Junction is located three miles north of Nacogdoches, and the Jacksonville Branch to Dallas diverges to the right at the switch behind the block signal. Most of the branch was abandoned in the 1980s; three segments are in service today (1.3 miles at Bonita Junction, 13.6 miles at Athens, and 6.0 miles near Dallas). (Tom Kline.)

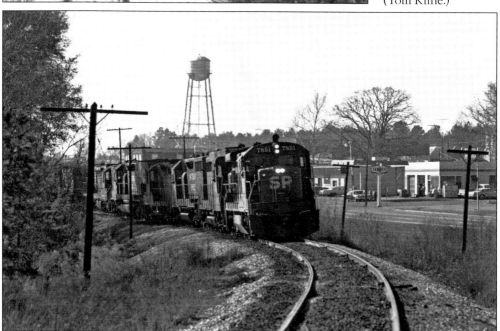

The steep 1.4-percent grade up Fitze Hill was too much for this Shreveport-bound freight train that had to "double the hill" on January 3, 1981, This involved dragging the train in two pieces to the siding at Garrison and putting it back together. The entire train is shown departing Garrison. (George Hamlin.)

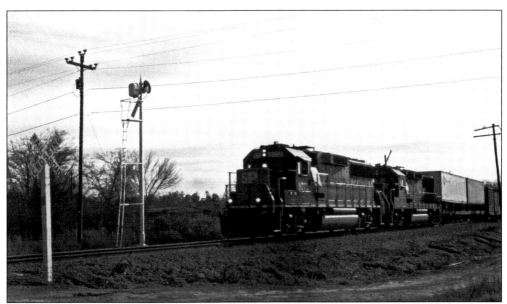

At Tenaha, located at milepost 176 on the Shreveport Subdivision, Southern Pacific crossed the Atchison, Topeka & Santa Fe Railway's line between Silsbee and Longview. The railroads maintained a joint station here and interchanged cars, primarily destined to and from the Texas Eastman chemical plant in Longview, which was also served by the Missouri Pacific Railroad. A cabin interlocking with semaphore signals was installed in 1927 to protect the crossing at grade. This interlocking was normally lined for Southern Pacific movements and would be manually operated by a Santa Fe crewmember for their trains. In 1982, it was converted to an automatic interlocking, retaining the semaphore signals on each railroad. These photographs show a westward SP train crossing the Santa Fe on March 3, 1994. Southern Pacific began replacing cabooses with electronic end-of-train devices in June 1984. (Tom Kline.)

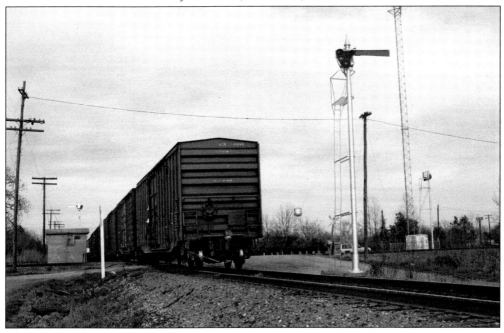

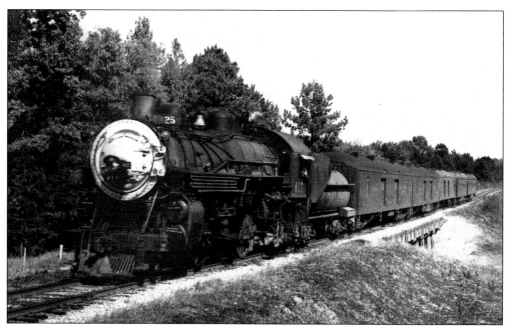

Houston-bound Train No. 25 hauled by aging Pacific Type locomotive No. 617 rolls through Keithville, Louisiana, in 1954. The locomotive was scrapped in May and the train discontinued in September 1954. (Harold K. Vollrath.)

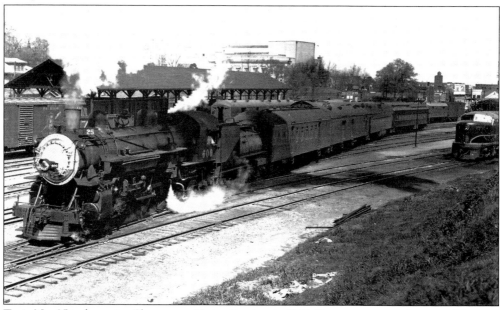

Train No. 25 is departing Shreveport Union Station in 1952. Passenger service between Houston and Shreveport commenced on January 30, 1886, and prior to 1905, Southern Pacific trains were using the Kansas City Southern station in Shreveport. The station was remodeled in 1940 and renamed Union Station, with the Kansas City Southern Railway, Louisiana & Arkansas Railway, Illinois Central Railroad, St. Louis Southwestern Railway (Cotton Belt), and Southern Pacific as tenants. Southern Pacific trains operated over Kansas City Southern tracks for 0.9 mile to reach home rails. (Harold K. Vollrath.)

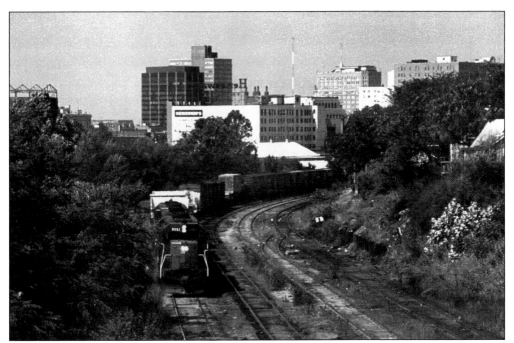

A Houston-bound freight train is departing Shreveport in November 1969 on Illinois Central's double-track line. Southern Pacific began using this route in 1934 to access Cotton Belt's yard. The two tracks on the right were owned by Kansas City Southern Railway, and the former Union Station at Louisiana Street was behind the train beyond the curve. (Steve Standifer.)

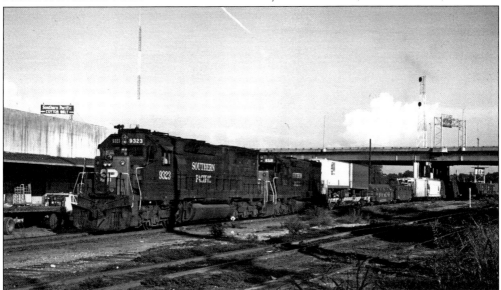

Departing from Cotton Belt's Shreveport Yard on August 25, 1977, a Houston-bound freight train is passing under Interstate 20 and approaching the Spring Street connection to the Illinois Central Railroad (IC). In 1934, Southern Pacific freight trains began originating and terminating at the Cotton Belt yard instead of the SP yard at mile post 231 and utilized 1.3 miles of IC track between Jordan Street and Spring Street. The locomotive is passing the joint SP and Cotton Belt freight station. (Mike Palmieri.)

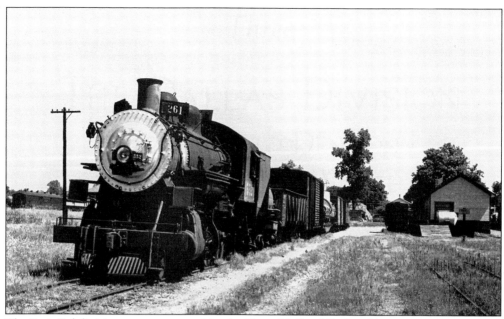

The Paris Subdivision was constructed by the Texas Midland Railroad between 1894 and 1896, and purchased by Southern Pacific on April 1, 1928. By the time these photographs were taken in 1948, 30.3 miles between Ennis and Kaufman had been abandoned due to the floods on March 19, 1942, which washed out the railroad in 13 locations. Subsequent abandonments occurred in 1958 between Kaufman and Greenville, in 1975 between Commerce and Paris, and in 1983 in Paris. Passenger service ended on May 11, 1941. Train No. 261 was the local freight train operating between Paris and Kaufman six days per week. In the above image, No. 261 is preparing to depart Paris. Below, the train is approaching Terrell. (Roger S. Plummer courtesy of Gordon Bassett.)

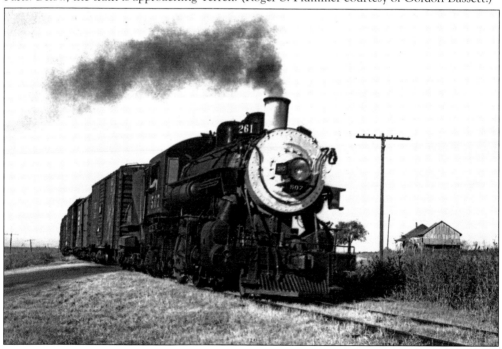

Three
THE DALLAS DIVISION
HOUSTON TO DENISON
ENNIS TO FORT WORTH

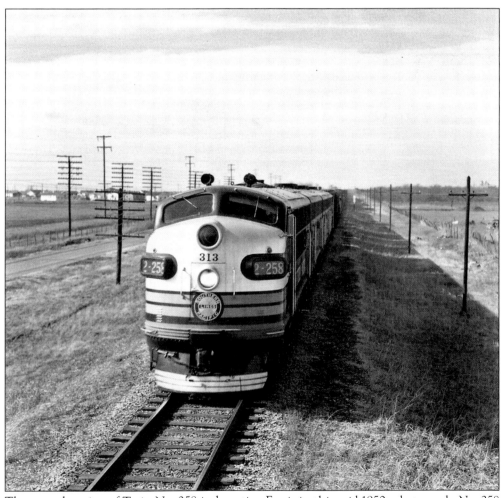

The second section of Train No. 258 is departing Ennis in this mid-1950s photograph. No. 258 operated daily between Ennis and Englewood Yard in Houston, a distance of 233 miles. (John Signor Collection.)

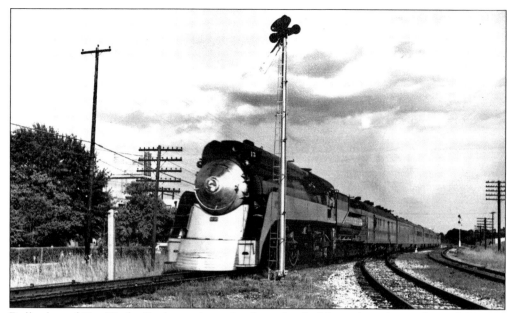

Dallas-bound No. 13, the Sunbeam, is passing from the double track to the single-track Hearne Subdivision at Eureka in July 1948. Eureka is located five miles northwest of the Houston passenger station, and the single arm semaphore signal in the foreground indicates No. 13 will not receive any train orders today at Tower 13, which is located behind the photographer. The tracks curving to the right are the Houston–San Antonio main line. (Dr. Phillip Hastings courtesy of the California State Railroad Museum, Sacramento, California.)

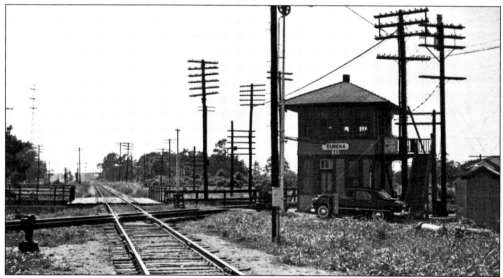

This view of Tower 13 at Eureka is facing west toward Smithville on the Missouri-Kansas-Texas Railroad with the Hearne Subdivision crossing in the foreground. The tower was placed in service July 5, 1903, and initially protected this crossing, and later the junction between T&NOs main line and the Hearne Subdivision was added. Tower 13 assumed control of the interlockings at West Junction (1931), Boulevard Junction (1940), and Bellaire Junction (1945). The tower was closed in 1966, and its functions were transferred to Tower 26. (Joe R. Thompson courtesy of the Railroad and Heritage Museum, Temple, Texas.)

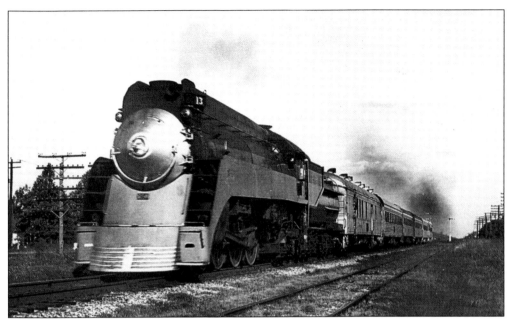

The outbound Sunbeam is high stepping through Fairbanks in northwest Houston around 1949. Southern Pacific rebuilt and streamlined three Pacific Type locomotives (650–652) for Sunbeam service at the Houston shops in 1937. During 1949, Southern Pacific began operating Alco PA-1 diesel locomotives on the Sunbeam and Hustler, although steam locomotives were also used through 1954. No. 652 was scrapped in December 1952, and locomotives 650 and 651 were sold for scrap in March 1954. (Harold K. Vollrath.)

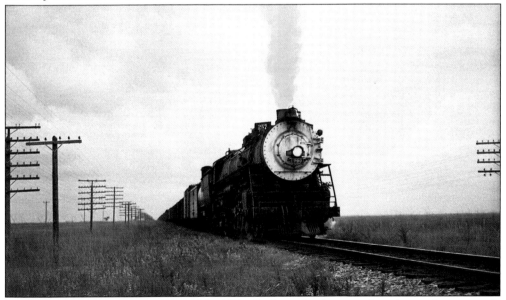

Pictured in 1952, Ennis-bound Train No. 257 rolls through what was then the rural countryside between Eureka and Cypress. General Service Type 4-8-4 locomotive No. 700 works to maintain the 60 miles per hour maximum speed for freight trains. Streamlined passenger trains operated at 79 miles per hour with diesel power and 75 miles per hour with steam power. (Joe R. Thompson courtesy of the Railroad and Heritage Museum, Temple, Texas.)

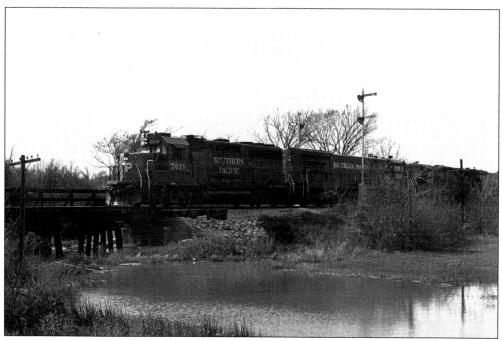

A westward freight train en route to Houston passes the semaphore signals at the west end of the Cypress siding, 20 miles east of Eureka, on February 24, 1980. The 5,390-foot siding was the first location outside Houston to meet trains on the Hearne Subdivision. This train waited at Cypress for several hours to meet a train from Houston. (George W. Hamlin.)

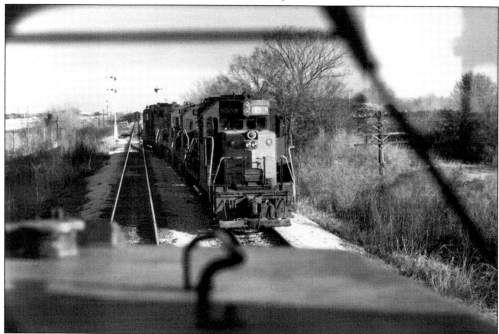

An eastward train led by GP35 No. 6508 has cut their power away from the train and is entering the siding at Cypress in March 1978 to swap locomotives with the Houston-bound train holding the main track. (Gary Morris.)

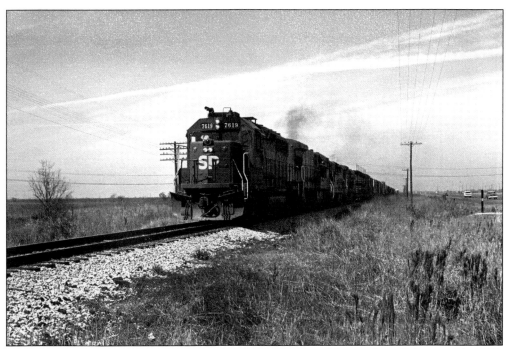

GP40 locomotive 7619 is leading train ENHOY (Ennis to Houston) on February 24, 1980, between Hockley and Cypress. This portion of the Hearne Subdivision was constructed by the Houston & Texas Central Railway Company during 1856 and 1857 as a 5-foot-6-inch broad-gauge railroad. In 1874, it was converted to the standard 4-foot-8½-inch gauge railroad. (George W. Hamlin.)

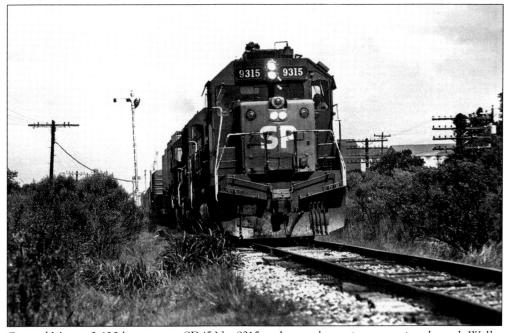

General Motors 3,600-horsepower SD45 No. 9315 and two other units are passing through Waller with a Hearne-bound freight train in July 1976. (Gary Morris.)

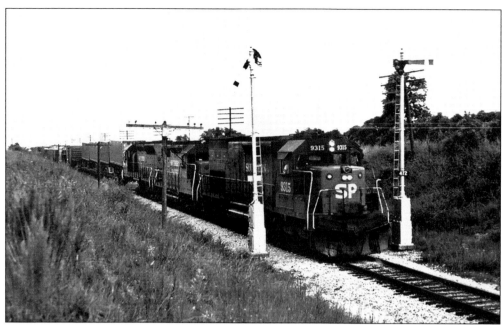

The Houston Division's Hearne Subdivision between Eureka and Hearne was the last significant location of semaphore signals on the Southern Pacific in Texas, many of them lasting into the 1980s before being replaced by color searchlight signals. In the June 1976 photograph above, train HODAT (Houston to Dallas) splits the semaphores between Waller and Hempstead. Below, the caboose of train ENHOY (Ennis to Houston) is passing the east switch at the Waller siding in March 1978. (Gary Morris.)

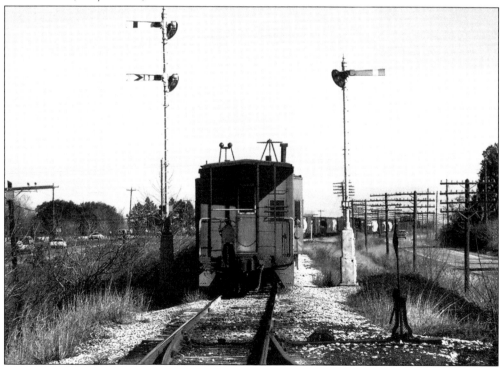

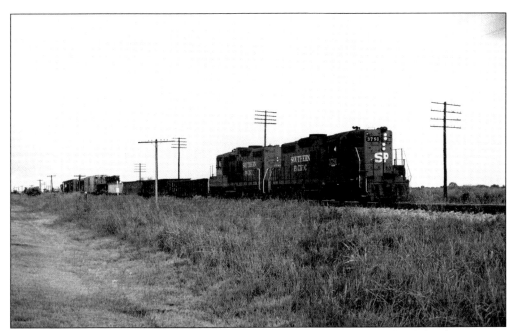

A pair of GP9 locomotives are hauling No. 55, the Houston to Hearne local freight train, on August 15, 1980. The location is Salt Mine Spur at milepost 33, where a 4.1-mile spur extended southward to a gypsum mine. (George W. Hamlin.)

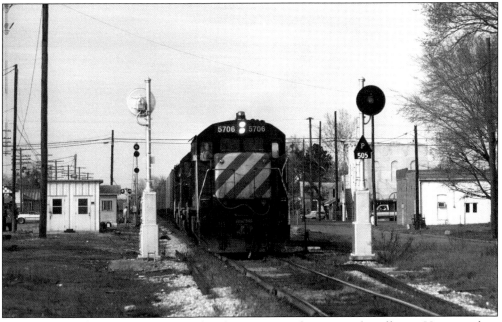

A westward Burlington Northern Railroad train passes the train order office at Hempstead on February 24, 1980. This train was detouring over Southern Pacific because of a derailment on Burlington Northern between Dallas and Houston. The triangular "P" plate on block signal 505 indicates this signal protects a special device, in this case the spring switch at the east end of the siding. The train order operator can be seen in the background inspecting the passing train. (George W. Hamlin.)

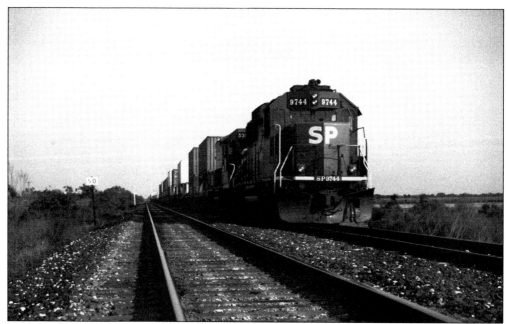

Train HODAT (Houston to Dallas) is easing down the siding at Hempstead for a meet with a westbound train on July 17, 1994. The tree line along the horizon in the right side of the photograph marks the former 115-mile line to Austin that was abandoned between Hempstead and Chappell Hill in 1961 and between Chappel Hill and Brenham in 1962. (Tom Kline.)

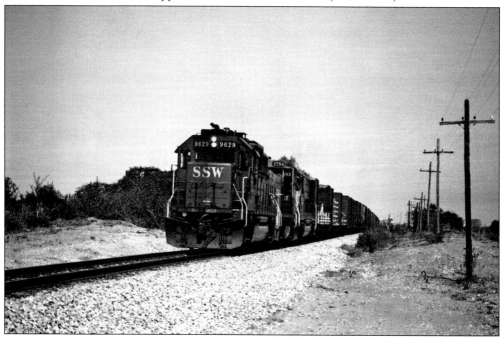

It is already 95 degrees at 11:03 a.m. on August 20, 1993, as train HEHOM (Hearne to Englewood Yard, Houston) leaves Millican. Visible in the background is the American Plant Food plant, which was served by rail. Construction of the Houston & Texas Central Railway halted from March 1860 until February 1867 at Millican. (David M. Bernstein.)

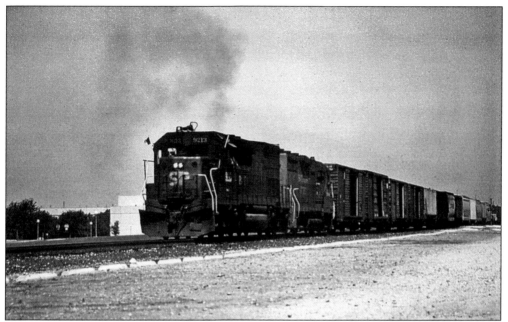

Train FWHOM (Fort Worth to Englewood Yard, Houston) bisects the campus of Texas A&M University at College Station on the morning of April 20, 1991. Engineer Ted Hollingshead is displaying American flags on locomotive 9213 as a tribute to servicemen fighting in Iraq during Operation Desert Storm. The train is hustling to Millican to meet train HOCHF (Houston to Chicago.) (David M. Bernstein.)

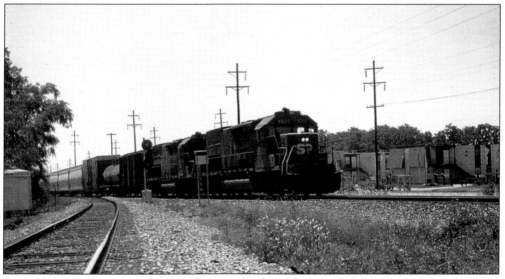

Train HOCHF (Houston to Chicago) is passing through Bryan Junction at 12:10 p.m. on April 20, 1991. The Missouri Pacific Railroad abandoned its line and began operating 27.8 miles over Southern Pacific's Hearne Subdivision between Navasota Junction and Bryan Junction on June 30, 1965. The track curving to the left is Missouri Pacific's main track to Bryan and Fort Worth. On January 9, 1992, the Union Pacific assumed maintenance and operation of the Hearne Subdivision between Navasota Junction and Bryan Junction (Union Pacific had purchased the Missouri Pacific in 1980). (David M. Bernstein.)

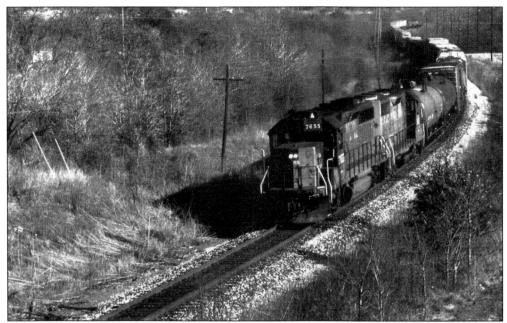

The second locomotive on train HOASQ (Houston to East St. Louis) has failed as it struggles out of Bryan toward Hearne on January 12, 1991. The rolling terrain and ascent to Sutton will provide a stiff challenge to 3,000-horsepower GP-40 No. 7655 hauling 45 loaded cars. This section of track between Benchley and Sutton was abandoned in September 1996 with the Union Pacific merger. The abandonment was vacated, and the line returned to service in 1998. (Tom Kline.)

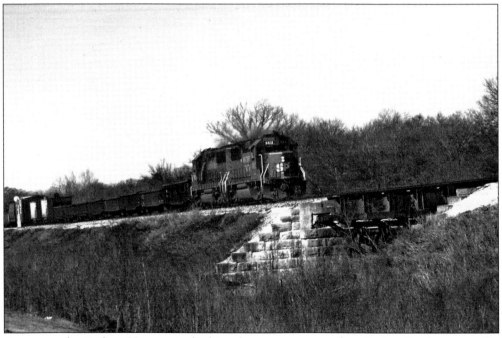

An eastward train from Houston is climbing the one-percent grade at Spring Creek, seven miles geographically south of Hearne on January 6, 1989. A one-percent grade is a one-foot rise in elevation over 100 feet of track. (Tom Kline.)

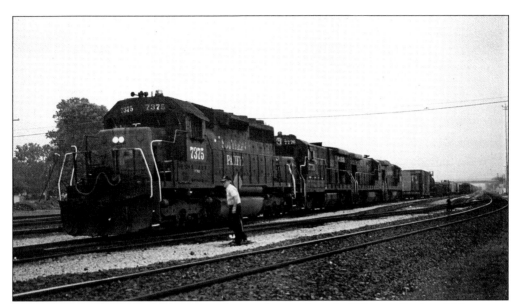

Conductor Stanley Liska is lining switches at the north end of Hearne Yard at 8:00 a.m. on March 27, 1991. Stanley's train HODAF (Houston to Dallas) has set out 94 cars and will depart with 37 cars. The track in the foreground is the Dalsa main track to Flatonia and San Antonio. (David M. Bernstein.)

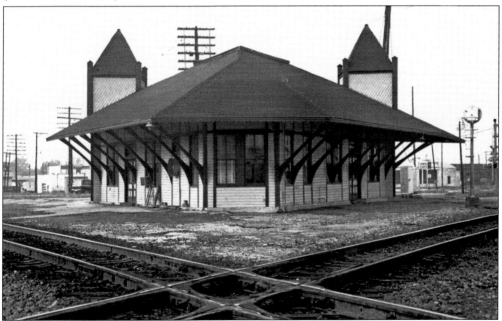

The Hearne passenger station was constructed in 1901 as a joint venture by the Houston & Texas Central Railroad (SP) and the International–Great Northern Railroad (later became Missouri Pacific Railroad). Tower 15 stood where the photographer is standing, and in 1935, it was closed when the interlocking machine protecting the crossing was moved into the station. When Southern Pacific ceased passenger train operations in 1958, the Missouri Pacific moved their passenger business into their freight station. The station was relocated in 2001 and is now a museum. (David M. Bernstein.)

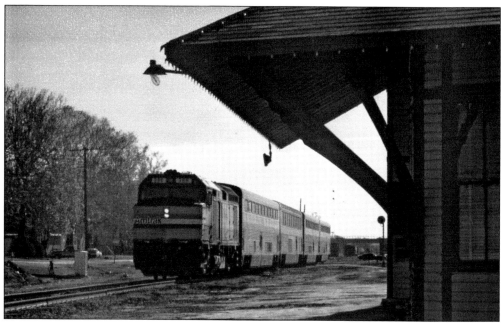

Amtrak Train No. 522, the Houston to Dallas section of the Texas Eagle, is shown rolling by the depot at Hearne on January 6, 1988. Amtrak originally planned to change the routing of the Texas Chief from the Santa Fe Railway to the SP between Houston and Dallas in 1973 but was unable to come to an agreement on track and signal upgrades required to operate passenger service. The Houston–Dallas section of the Texas Eagle operated from November 15, 1988, until termination due to budget cuts on September 10, 1995. (Tom Kline.)

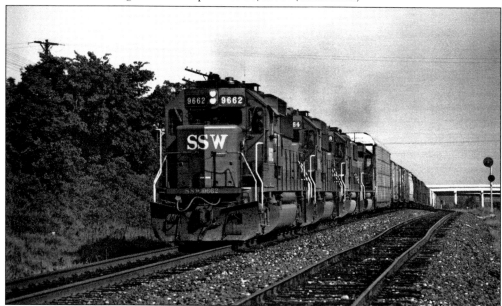

Train WCPBQ (West Colton, California, to Pine Bluff, Arkansas) blasts through Seger at 5:36 p.m. on May 28, 1993. The SSW on the nose indicates ownership by the St. Louis Southwestern Railway (Cotton Belt), which came under Southern Pacific control in 1932. Seger was the first siding north of Hearne. The bridge in the background carries U.S. Highway 79. (David M. Bernstein.)

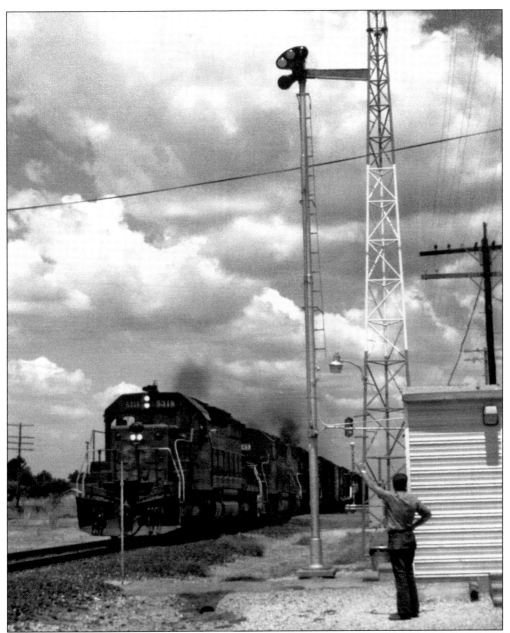

The train order operator at Bremond gives a friendly wave to the crew on an eastward (geographic southward) train en route to Hearne on August 19, 1978. Bremond is located 23 miles from Hearne and was the junction with a 45-mile branch line to Waco until it was abandoned in 1965. Note that the train order signal is for westward trains only because there was Centralized Traffic Control (CTC) between Bremond and Hearne, and train orders are not used for movement authority. CTC was installed between Hearne and Seger (four miles) in 1956 and extended 19 miles to Bremond in 1963. The practice was to issue westward trains en route to the Ennis Subdivision at Hearne train orders pertaining only to track conditions and issue train orders for movement authority at Bremond. This reduced the workload on the busy operator at Hearne, who copied train orders for three train dispatchers and operated the interlocking. (John Carr.)

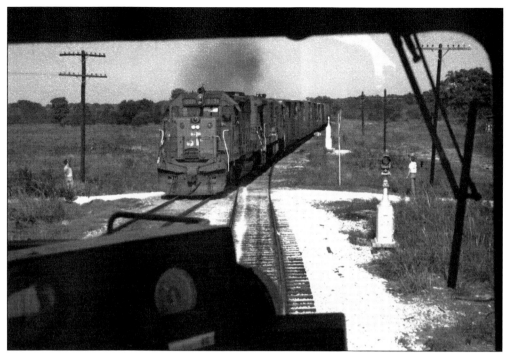

A 1980 meet at Groesbeck 40 miles south of Corsicana, as viewed from lead locomotive of train EMFWN (empty unit coal train). The head brakeman and fireman of the empty coal train are at the road crossing, watching train ENWCY (Ennis to West Colton, California) roll by. The empty coal train is en route from the City Public Service electricity generating plant at Elmendorf, south of San Antonio, to the Burlington Northern Railroad at Fort Worth for reloading in Wyoming. (John Carr.)

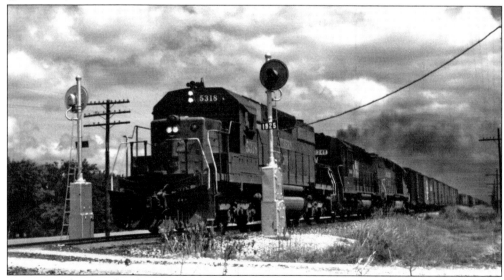

An eastward train splits the searchlight signals at milepost 192 between Richand and Wortham on August 19, 1978. The 2,300-horsepower SD39 No. 5319 is doing most of the work account the Norfolk & Western engine had electrical problems and the rear engine was overheating. (John Carr.)

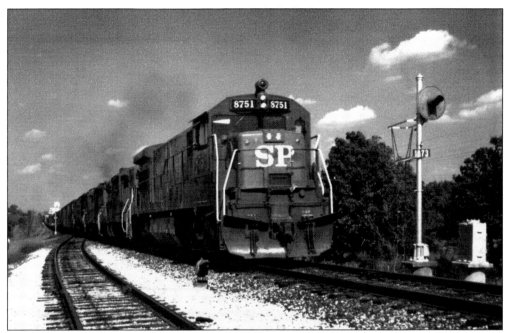

Train ENWCY (Ennis to West Colton, California) rolls by the west siding switch at Gude, two miles north of Wortham, in 1980. The short signal between the siding and main track is a dwarf signal with a low profile so that there are no clearance issues that a standard high signal would present. (John Carr.)

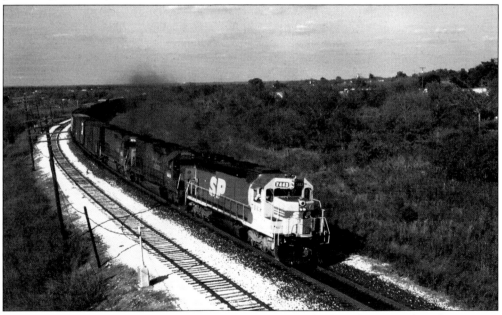

Train FWHOM (Fort Worth to Englewood Yard, Houston) had a colorful touch with unit 7443 in the Southern Pacific Santa Fe merger yellow and red paint scheme as it rounds a curve near Mexia in May 1987. Had the Interstate Commerce Commission not denied the merger between the two railroads in 1986, the letters SF would have been added following SP to spell SPSF. (Barry Byington Sr.)

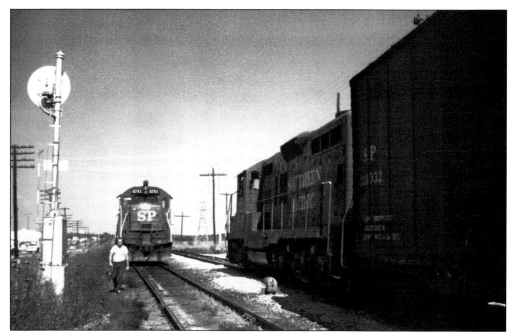

Train ENWCY (Ennis to West Colton, California) and No. 53, the Hearne to Ennis local, are meeting at the east (south) end of Corsicana siding in 1980. The ENWCY has stopped on the main track, and the head brakeman is walking ahead to line the siding switch for their movement after the local enters the siding. The meet was directed via written train orders transmitted by the train dispatcher at San Antonio to train order operators, who then delivered the orders to the train crews. (John Carr.)

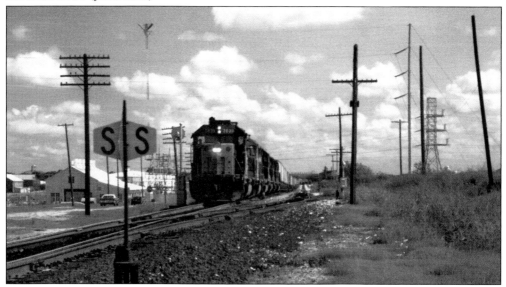

Expedited trains such as the BSMFF (Blue Streak Merchandise) and MBSMF (Memphis Blue Streak Merchandise) operated at 70 miles per hour on the 89-mile Corsicana to Hearne speedway and could make the run in less than 100 minutes. Train dispatchers were under pressure to see these trains were not delayed. In this photograph, the MBSMF (Memphis to Los Angeles) has completed the crew change and is departing Corsicana on June 21, 1986. (John Carr.)

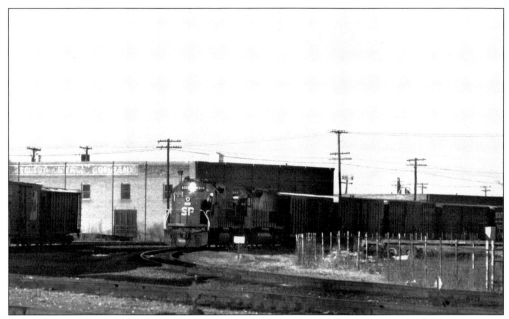

A freight train from the St. Louis Southwestern Railway (Cotton Belt) eases around the connecting track to the Ennis Subdivision at Corsicana in January 1977. Southern Pacific obtained control of the Cotton Belt in 1932, providing a vital link between St. Louis, Pine Bluff, and the SP at Corsicana. The Cotton Belt also linked with SP at Dallas, Fort Worth, Lufkin, Plano, Sherman, Shreveport, and Waco. (Tom Kline.)

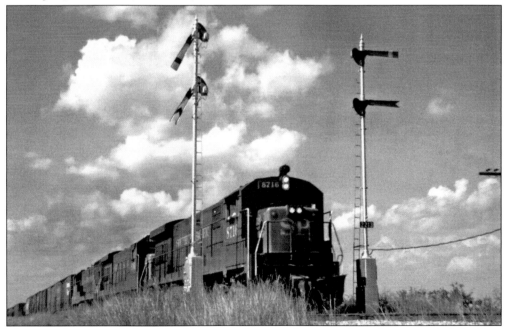

The second section of Train No. 260 passes the semaphore signals at the east end of the Rice siding. This was the only location between Ennis and Corsicana to meet or pass trains. The semaphore signals were replaced by color searchlight signals when the siding was lengthened from 3,564 feet long to 10,067 feet in 1982. (John Carr.)

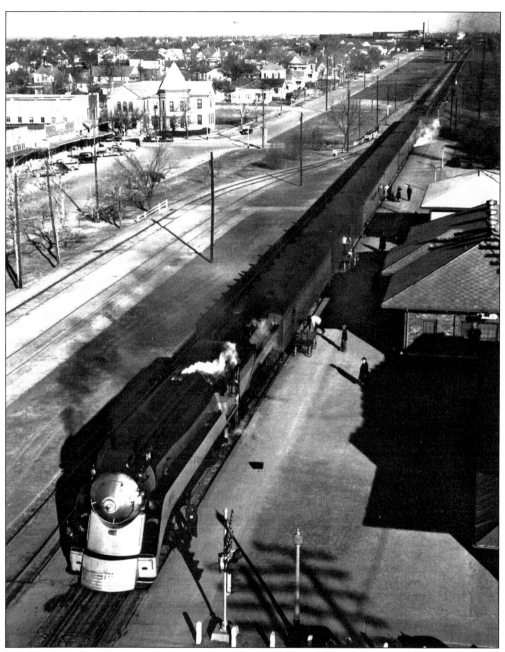

The Hustler calls at Ennis in 1948 en route to Houston's Grand Central Station. This train carried streamlined chair cars and a diner/lounge/observation car on a six-hour schedule with 11 regular stops and 15 flag stops. During the last two decades of passenger service, three pair of trains operated between Dallas and Houston. The morning trains were Nos. 15 and 16, the Hustler. The afternoon trains were Nos. 13 and 14, the Sunbeam, operating on a 4-hour, 25-minute schedule with only a flag stop at College Station and a crew change stop at Ennis. The overnight trains carrying coaches, sleeping cars, and mail were Nos. 17 and 18, the Owl. The building with the turret in the background at the corner of Baylor and Main Streets was the headquarters for Southern Pacific's Dallas and Austin Divisions until 1964. (J. Ford Curry courtesy of Dane Williams.)

No. 18, the Houston-bound Owl, makes its midnight stop at Ennis in this c. 1953 image. Diesel locomotives began hauling passenger trains between Dallas and Houston in 1949, although steam engines were used through 1954. (J. Ford Curry courtesy of Dane Williams.)

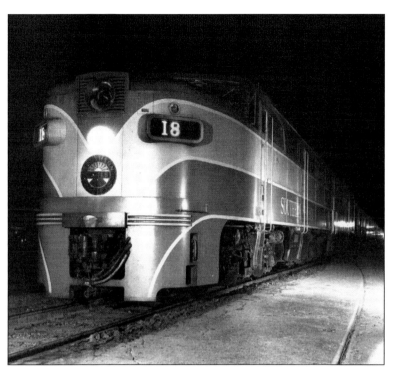

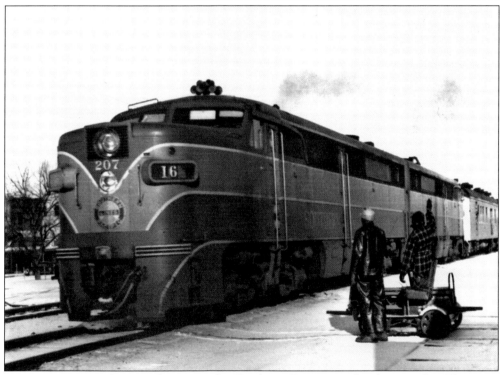

Two maintenance-of-way workers greet the Hustler in Ennis on a frigid winter day. They were waiting for the passenger train to depart before setting their gasoline-powered motor car on the track. (J. Ford Curry courtesy of Dane Williams.)

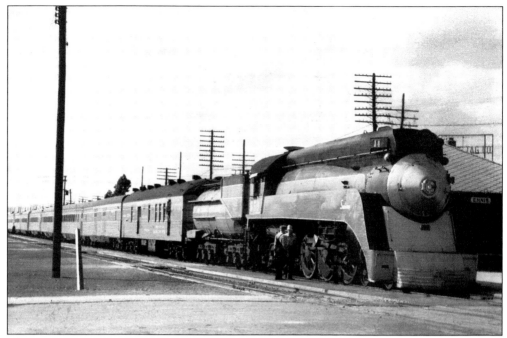

The Houston-bound Sunbeam makes its 5:40 p.m. stop at Ennis to change engine crews and entrain passengers in June 1947. Due to the short time spent at the station, no checked baggage was handled on the Sunbeam at Ennis (passengers could check baggage to be handled on other trains). The Sunbeam also made a flag stop at College Station with no checked baggage service. After the Hustler was discontinued in 1954, flag stops were added at Hearne, Bremond, and Corsicana. (J. Ford Curry courtesy of Dane Williams.)

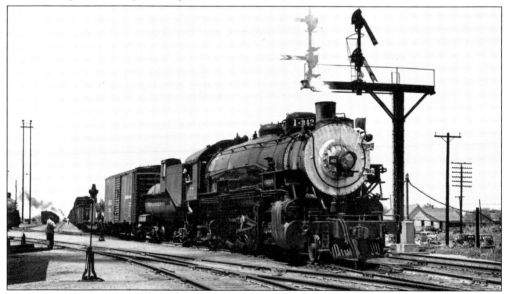

The first section of Train No. 342 is switching at the east end of Ennis yard in 1949. No. 342 operated daily from Denison to Englewood Yard in Houston. Engine 957 is displaying green flags, indicating at least one more section of No. 342 will follow. At night, green lights will be displayed instead of flags. (Roger S. Plummer courtesy of Gordon Bassett.)

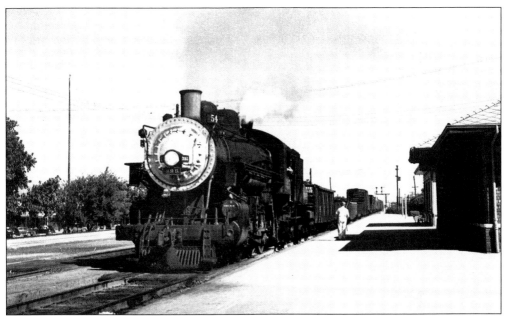

Ten Wheeler Type locomotive No. 395 prepares to depart Ennis with Train No. 54, the Ennis to Hearne local freight train in 1950. It will take No. 54 at least seven hours to cover the 110 miles to Hearne. In addition to picking up and setting out freight cars, No. 54 has to clear Nos. 15 and 16, the Hustlers, freight trains Nos. 342, 344, and 263, and any sections thereof, all of which are superior to No. 54. Also, there will be extra trains not shown in the employee timetable to deal with, as directed by train orders. (Roger S. Plummer courtesy of Gordon Bassett.)

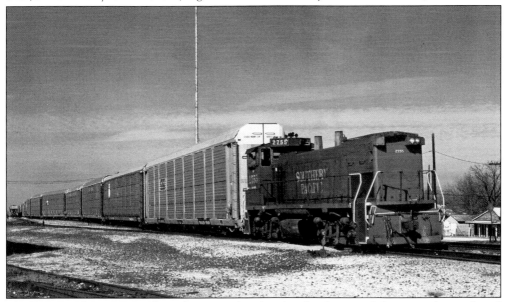

The Ennis yard engine switches a long cut of enclosed tri-level automobile cars at the south end of the yard on July 21, 1990. Establishment of the 165-acre auto unloading facility for Nissan and Mazda vehicles at Midlothian in the 1980s provided SP considerable revenue. Other major customers served from Ennis included Elk Roofing at Ennis and Chaparral Steel in Midlothian. (David M. Bernstein Collection.)

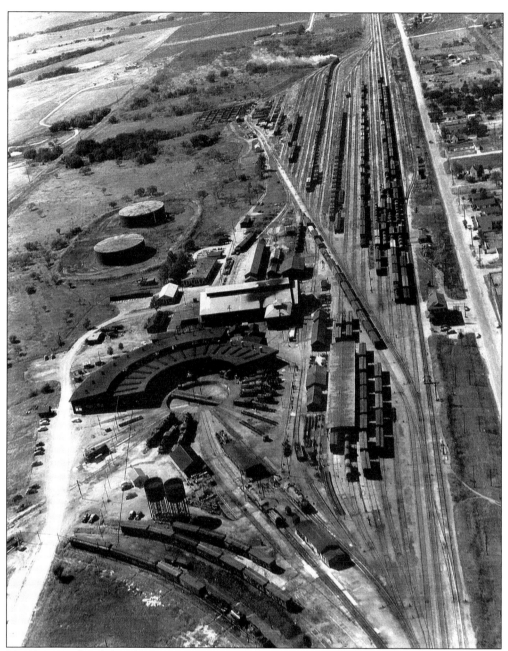

The Ennis yard and shop facilities are viewed looking northward in August 1948. The yard complex had 88,168 feet of track at the time. The shops included a 100-foot turntable, 15-stall roundhouse, wheel shop, fueling facilities, and repair facilities. Ennis was established by the Houston & Texas Central Railway, which purchased 647 acres of land there in 1871. The city agreed to provide the railroad with water, and the railroad agreed to keep the shops in Ennis as long as water was provided. There was a train dispatching office in Ennis until 1959, and a divisional headquarters until 1964. Southern Pacific was a major employer. Even as late as 1964, after the shops closed, over 300 railroaders resided in Ennis. The two-story building in the right margin of the photograph was the yard office. (J. Ford Curry courtesy of Dane Williams.)

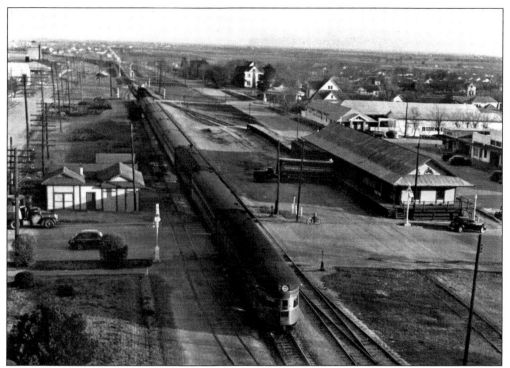

The Sunbeam has just departed the Ennis passenger station for Houston in this 1948 aerial view facing railroad east (geographic south). The large building on the right was the Ennis freight station at the corner of Brown Street and South Main Street. Note the Southern Pacific Transport Company truck spotted at the freight station. (J. Ford Curry courtesy of Dane Williams.)

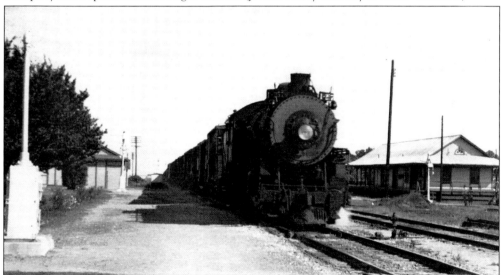

The first section of Train No. 247 from Houston is passing the wigwag crossing signals at Brown Street in Ennis. The Ennis freight station is to the right of the train. The head brakeman is leaving the doghouse on locomotive No. 743s tender to line the switch in preparation of entering Ennis yard about half of a mile ahead. Today the fright station no longer exists and the wigwag signals have been replaced by flashers and gates. (J. Ford Curry courtesy of Dane Williams.)

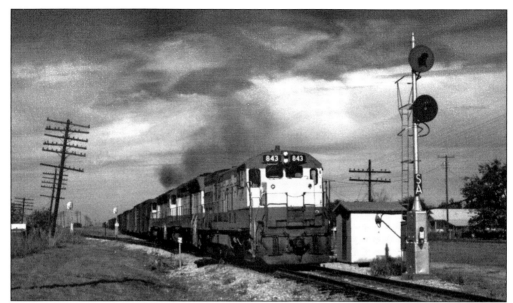

Three orange and white St. Louis–San Francisco Railway (Frisco) locomotives power a eastward train at Garrett on November 1, 1980. This was a run-through train from the Frisco delivered to Southern Pacific at Denison. The merger of the Frisco with the Burlington Northern is 20 days away, and following the merger, the run through traffic through Denison ended. Garrett is the junction of the Ennis Subdivision main line with the 54-mile Fort Worth Branch diverging to the north in the photograph. A power switch controlled by the operator at Ennis was installed at Garrett in 1928. In the picture below, engineers exchange greetings as the same Frisco run-through train meets a Dallas-bound train at Ferris, 13 miles west of Garrett. Ferris was the only siding between Ennis and Dallas Miller Yard at that time. (John Carr.)

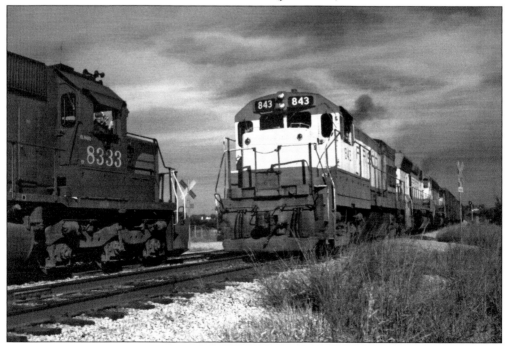

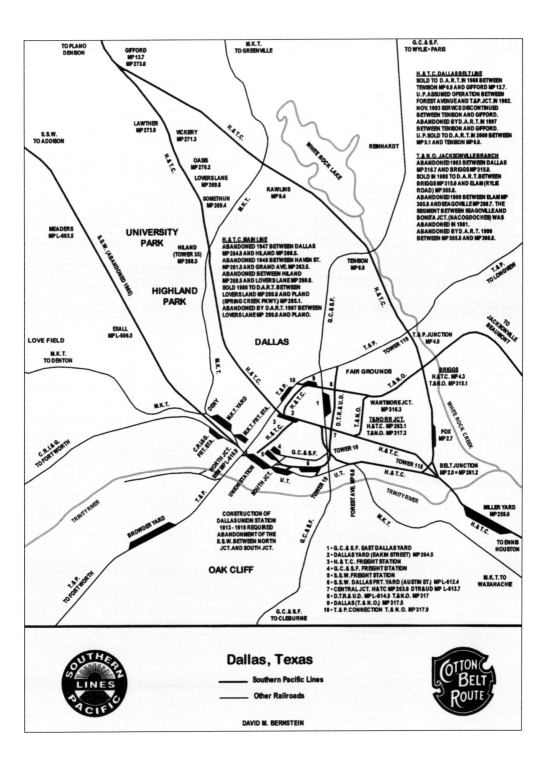

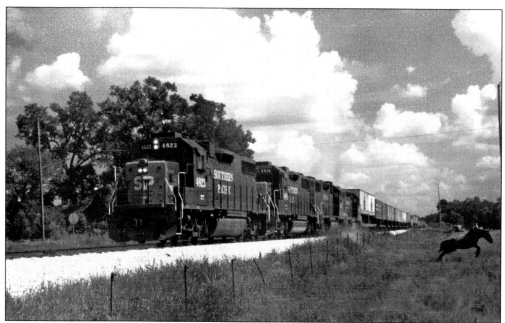

Train LADAF (Los Angeles to Dallas) disturbs the tranquility of the countryside near Trumbull, 25 miles south of Dallas on June 21, 1986. The approaching train spooked a horse grazing near the tracks on the railroad side of the fence, causing the horse to jump the fence. (John Carr.)

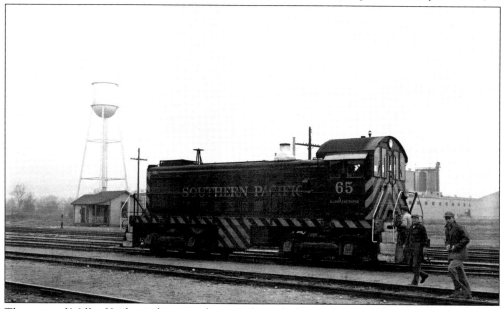

The crew of Miller Yard switch engine hurries through the yard on a cold and foggy March day in 1959. Miller was the primary Southern Pacific yard in Dallas with 11 classification tracks at an aggregate length of 38,133 feet, a five-stall roundhouse, and turntable at that time. The St. Louis Southwestern Railway (Cotton Belt) began using Miller Yard in December 1965 after most of their line between Addison and Dallas was abandoned for construction of the Dallas North Tollway. The Cotton Belt then reached Dallas from Plano via the SP. (Dean Hale courtesy of the Railroad and Heritage Museum, Temple, Texas.)

These photographs offer two views of the north end of Miller Yard in Dallas, taken a generation apart. In the right photograph, Alco S-4 locomotive No. 99 is switching cars in the siding during 1959 at semaphore signal 2596 (259.6 miles from Houston). In hte photograph below, taken on June 21, 1995, train LADAF has just arrived Miller Yard from Los Angeles and is preparing to spot their cars at the intermodal facility. Note the replacement of the semaphore signals with color searchlight signals and the additional tracks constructed during the 26 years between photographs. (Right; Dean Hale courtesy of the Railroad and Heritage Museum, Temple; Below, John Carr.)

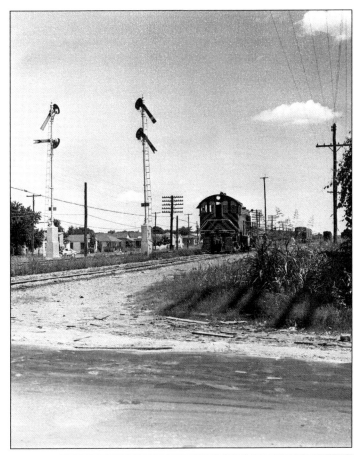

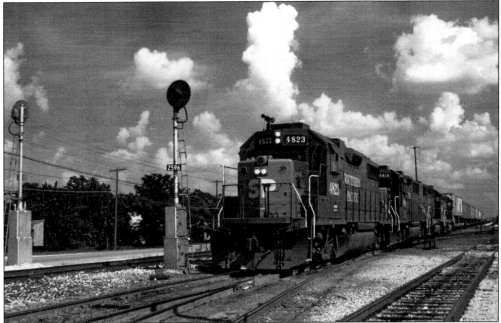

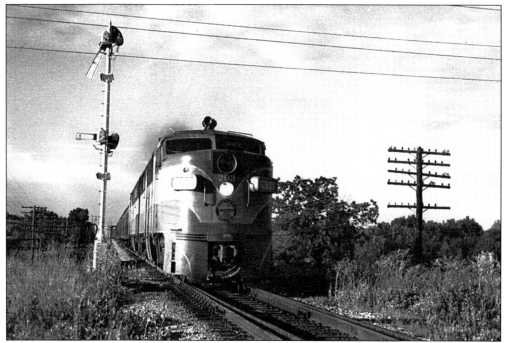

Overnight Train No. 17, the Owl from Houston, enters Dallas early in the morning of June 22, 1952. The Owl carried a sleeping car, coaches, and head end cars with mail, newspapers, express, and baggage. Through sleeping cars were handled between Galveston and Dallas, New Orleans and Denver, and between Houston and Fort Worth. (Roger S. Plummer courtesy of Gordon Bassett.)

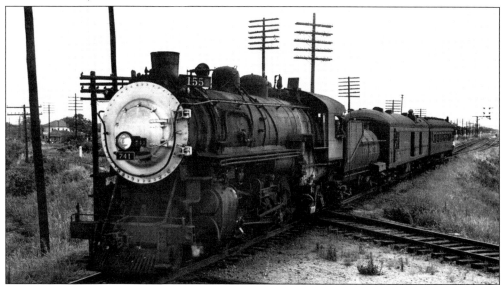

Seen above, Train No. 155 is passing through Belt Junction en route to Dallas Union Station on June 22, 1952. Train 155 was a mixed train from Beaumont via Nacogdoches and Jacksonville. It dropped off its freight cars at the Fox siding, out of sight just behind the coach, which will be picked up by a switch engine from Miller Yard. (Roger S. Plummer photograph courtesy of Gordon Bassett.)

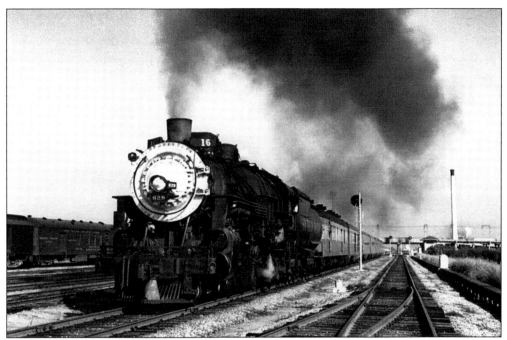

Pacific Type No. 628 leads the Hustler out of Dallas in 1950. The train is passing the Union Terminal Company coach yard south of the station. Visible in the background is the interurban viaduct and Dallas Union Terminal South Tower. (Roger S. Plummer courtesy of Gordon Bassett.)

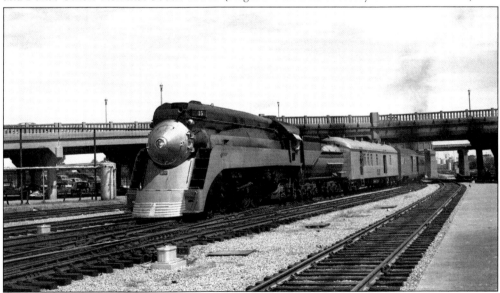

Train No. 15, the Hustler, is arriving at Dallas Union Station from Houston on the afternoon of August 11, 1951. The train is passing under the interurban viaduct and the Houston Street Viaduct (foreground) at the south end of the station. Southern Pacific passenger trains operated over two miles of double track between Belt Junction and Forest Avenue, 0.3 miles over the Missouri–Kansas–Texas Railroad from Forest Avenue to east limits of the Tower 19 interlocking, then 1.5 miles on the Union Terminal Company to the station. (Joe R. Thompson courtesy of the Railroad and Heritage Museum, Temple, Texas.)

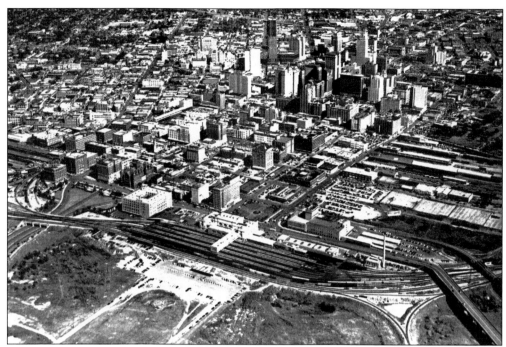

Above is an aerial view of downtown Dallas in the 1950s with Dallas Union Station in the foreground. In 1909, the Railroad Commission of Texas ordered construction of a union station in Dallas. The Union Terminal Company was chartered in 1912, with the eight railroads serving Dallas each owning 12.5 percent of the company. Construction began in January 1914 and was completed in three years. New yards, interlockings, bridges, and station facilities were built at a cost of $6.5 million ($143 million in 2010 dollars). Dallas Union Station opened for business in October 1916, replacing five passenger stations. The station was remodeled in 1948 and 1949, including access to trains by a tunnel and ramps from the ground floor, which replaced access from the second floor concourse and its long stairway. Below, the Hustler prepares for its 8:10 a.m. departure in 1950. (Above, Southern Pacific; below, Roger S. Plummer courtesy of Gordon Bassett.)

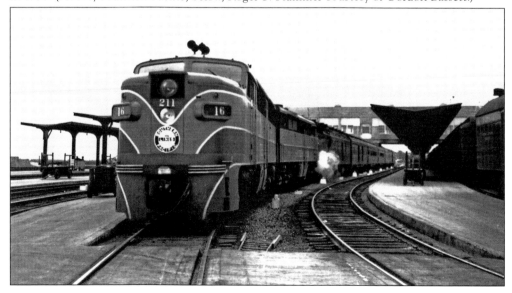

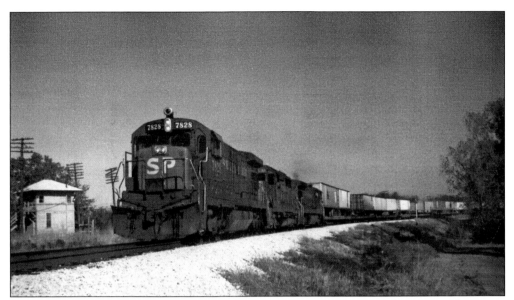

Building a belt line around Dallas had been proposed as early as 1906. The first 5-mile section from Forest Avenue to T&P Junction was completed in 1920 to provide direct access to Dallas Union Station and for Texas & Pacific Railway trains to bypass their original main line on Pacific Avenue. The nine-mile segment between T&P Junction and Gifford was completed in 1926, thereafter Southern Pacific through trains were rerouted from the old main line between downtown Dallas and Gifford (the old main line remained in place until the late 1940s when the right of way was sold for construction of the Central Expressway). Train ESDAQ (East St. Louis to Dallas) is shown above passing Tower 118 at Belt Junction en route to Miller Yard on November 21, 1987. Below, Rock Island No. 4311 leads Missouri Pacific Train NF (North Little Rock–Fort Worth) viewed from Tower 118 at Belt Junction on November 1, 1980. The track curving to the right leads to Miller Yard. Beyond the crossover is the Fox siding. (John Carr.)

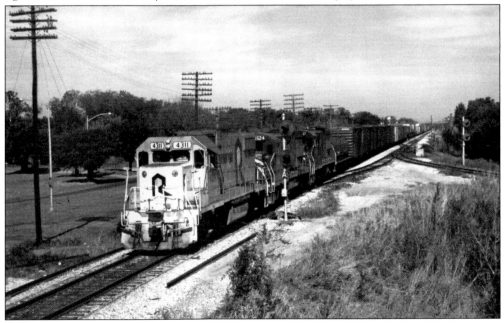

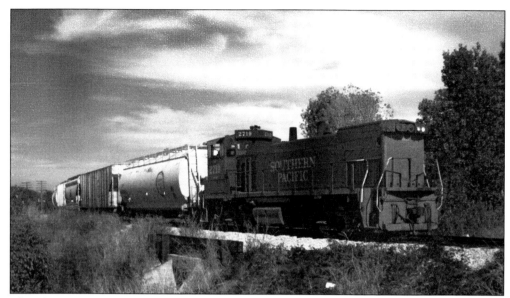

The Plano Turn has just passed Belt Junction and is about to cross the Trinity River Bridge en route to Miller Yard on November 1, 1980. Southern Pacific sold this line between Tenison Park (two miles north of MP Junction) and Plano to Dallas Area Rapid Transit in 1988 but continued operating over it until 1993. Effective December 6, 1993, the Carrollton Turn began operating between Dallas and Carrollton over the former Missouri-Kansas-Texas Railroad Denton Subdivision. (John Carr.)

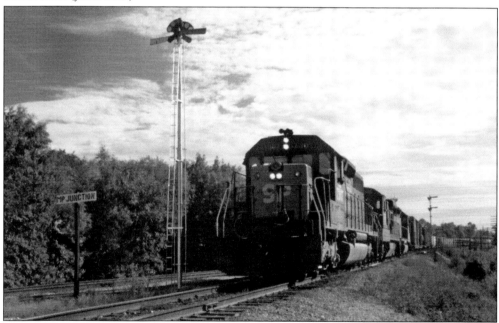

T&P Junction was renamed MP Junction in 1978. In the image above, Train ENDNY (Ennis to Denison) is passing the train order signal at MP Junction on November 1, 1980, and will pick up train orders at Tower 119, located behind the photographer. The connection to the Missouri Pacific line to Longview is on the opposite site of the train order signal. Tower 119 was closed in 1989. (John Carr.)

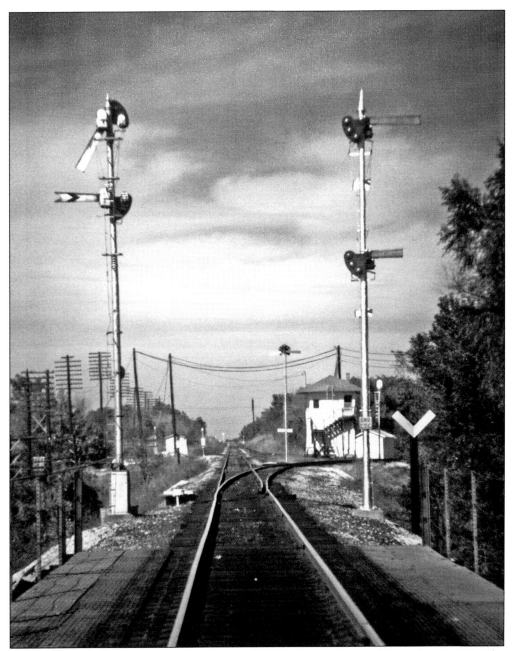

This view of MP Junction facing north toward Gifford was taken on November 1, 1980. The operator at Tower 119 has the switch lined for a Missouri Pacific train en route to Dallas. The Missouri Pacific crossed the Ennis Subdivision at the white instrument case just beyond the tower. The operator copied train orders for both railroads, controlled the interlocking, and controlled the Centralized Traffic Control between Briggs and MP Junction. Briggs was 0.8 mile south of MP Junction at the connection to the Athens Branch to Jacksonville. The Centralized Traffic Control from but excluding Briggs to Miller Yard was controlled by the Tower 118 operator at Belt Junction. The yellow "Y" shaped sign indicates the beginning of yard limits on the Southern Pacific at the end of Centralized Traffic Control. (John Carr.)

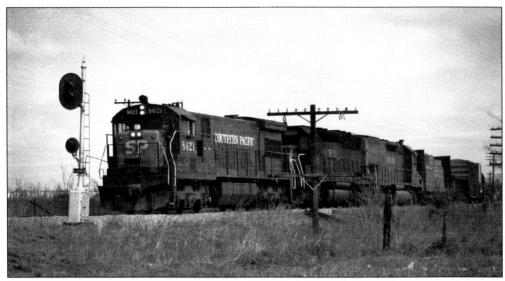

Train DNENY (Denison to Ennis) is rounding a curve near milepost 281 between Plano and Richardson on March 1, 1980. The signal D-2815 is the distant signal for the interlocking at the Cotton Belt crossing at Plano. When the signal displays a green aspect, trains approaching Plano will expect a green interlocking signal, and when yellow is displayed, they will expect a red (stop) signal at the interlocking. (Jimmy Barlow.)

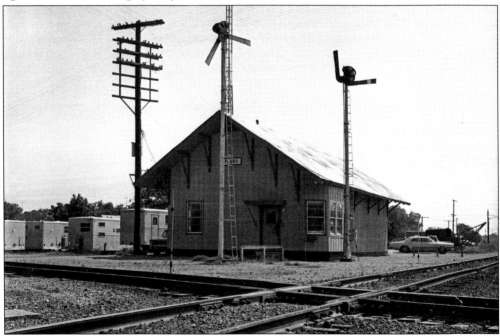

The joint Southern Pacific–Cotton Belt station at Plano was located at the crossing of the two railroads south of downtown. Although both railroads had common ownership, they used different operating rule books until 1985, hence the lower quadrant semaphore train order signals governing SP and the upper-quadrant type governing Cotton Belt trains. This view is looking eastward on the Cotton Belt in 1966. (Dean Hale courtesy of the Railroad and Heritage Museum, Temple, Texas.)

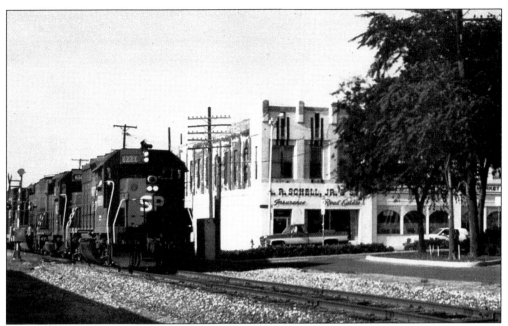

A Dallas-bound train crosses East Fifteenth Street in downtown Plano on August 26, 1985. Southern Pacific sold this line between the Santa Fe Railway overpass at Tenison Park (mile post 6.9) and Spring Creek Parkway to Dallas Area Rapid Transit (DART) in April 1988. Also included in the $58-million sale was 14 miles of other trackage in the Dallas area. The last SP train operated through downtown Plano on the evening of December 6, 1993. Today this is the double track DART Red Line. (Jimmy Barlow.)

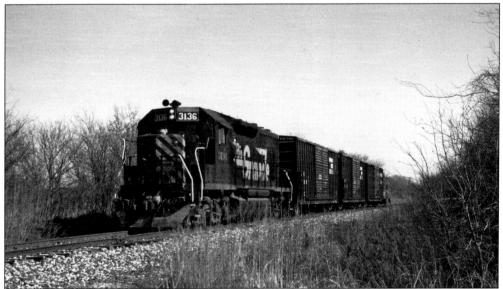

The 3,000-horsepower Denver & Rio Grande Western Railroad GP40 No. 3136 has no problem handling the three cars and caboose of the Sherman Local north of McKinney on March 23, 1995. Southern Pacific merged with the Denver & Rio Grande Western in 1988. The Dallas, Garland & Northeastern Railroad leased this line from Plano to South Sherman Junction in January 1999. (Jimmy Barlow.)

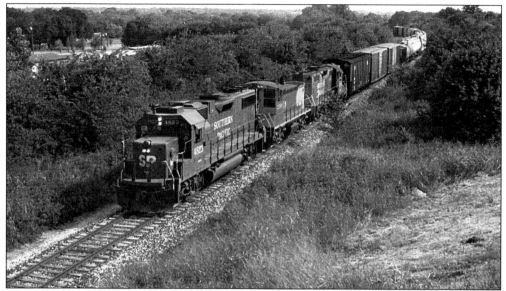

The Ennis to Denison Local rolls through the rural Collin County countryside near Melissa on the afternoon of July 22, 1987. After the merger of the St. Louis–San Francisco Railway (Frisco) and the Burlington Northern Railroad in 1980, traffic north of Plano was handled by local freight trains. Most of the interchange at Denison ceased, since Burlington Northern would long haul traffic instead of sharing revenue with Southern Pacific. (Jimmy Barlow.)

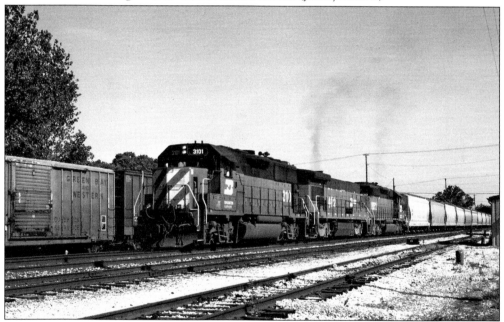

Above, Burlington Northern Train No. 152 (Houston to Galesburg, Illinois) is passing Southern Pacific's Sherman yard on May 16, 1996. BN predecessor St. Louis– San Francisco Railway obtained trackage rights between Sherman and Denison in 1900, and later extended them to South Sherman Junction. Burlington Northern purchased the 13.5-mile line from Denison to South Sherman Junction from SP for $2.3 million in 1993. SP was granted 3.9 miles of trackage rights from South Sherman Junction to Sherman. (Jimmy Barlow.)

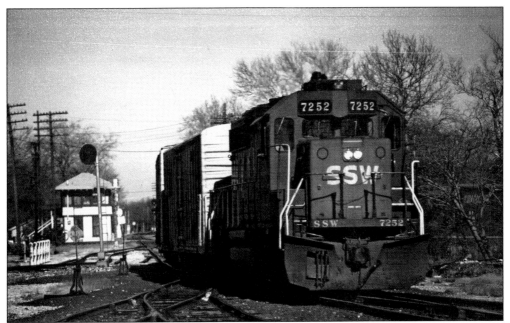

In this image, Cotton Belt GP-40-2 locomotive No. 7252 has arrived in Sherman with two cars on January 12, 1991. Tower 16 in the background is where the Texas Northeastern Railroad (TNER) crossed the Southern Pacific. The TNER line was the Missouri Pacific line between Whitesboro and Texarkana, which TNER leased in 1990. Tower 16 also controlled the Centralized Traffic Control on the SP between Denison and Sherman (8.3 miles) and between Frisco Junction and South Sherman Junction (2.1 miles). The tower closed on October 22, 2001, and is now on display at the Grapevine Vintage Railroad in Grapevine. (Jimmy Barlow.)

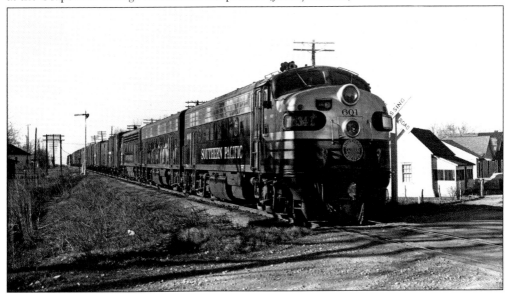

The first section of Train 341 (Denison to Houston's Englewood Yard) is passing through Sherman in February 1958. The photograph was labeled as "McKinney;" however, there were no automatic block signals in McKinney and aerial photographs indicate the location is probably the northern section of Sherman. Block signals were installed between Denison and Sherman in 1946. (Jim Shaw.)

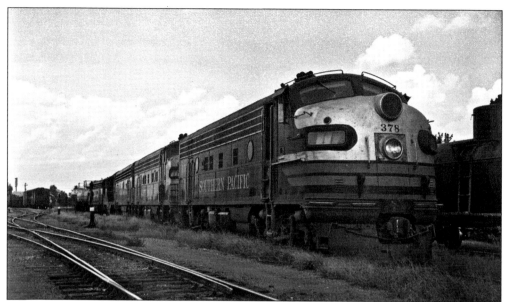

An eastward train at Denison prepares to depart for its 106-mile run to Ennis on September 16, 1960. Southern Pacific had considerable interchange with the Missouri–Kansas–Texas Railroad and St. Louis–San Francisco Railway at Denison. Passenger service ceased in 1935 between Dallas and Denison. This line originally terminated 3.7 miles north of Denison at Red River City, abandoned in 1876. (A. Dean Hale courtesy of the Railroad and Heritage Museum, Temple, Texas.)

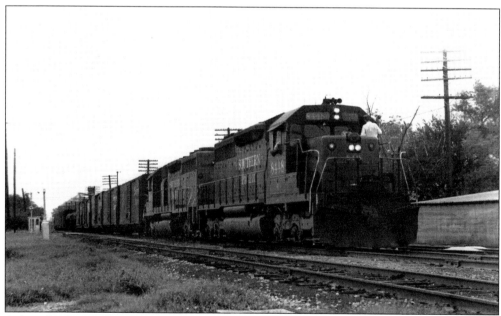

A short freight train has just arrived Denison in September 1971. With the reduction of interchange traffic at Denison beginning in the early 1980s, Southern Pacific was left essentially with local business only. Southern Pacific operations between Sherman and Denison ended in 1991 when the Texas Northeastern Railroad began serving SP customers under a cooperative marketing agreement. (Jim Shaw.)

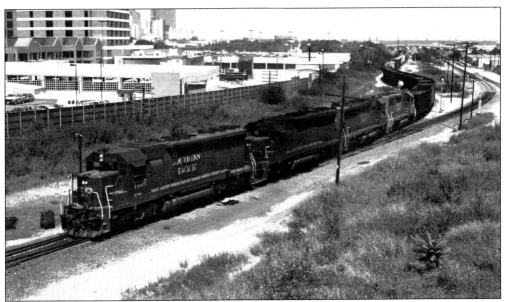

Outbound from Broadway Yard in Fort Worth on August 29, 1980, an eastward Southern Pacific freight train negotiates the two power switches on and off the Atchison, Topeka & Santa Fe Railway at the former location of Tower 126. The two railroads crossed here until 1961 when they built new connections, retired the crossing, and closed the tower. The Santa Fe train dispatcher assumed control when the tower was retired. The Santa Fe Railway referred to this location as Polks. (Jimmy Barlow.)

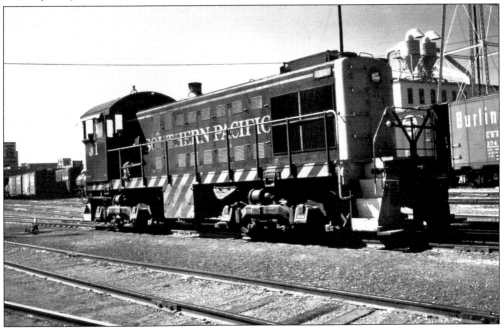

Twenty-one-year-old Alco S2 switch engine No. 31 rests between assignments at Fort Worth's Broadway Yard in June 1964. From the cramped yard, Southern Pacific managed to interchange cars with eight railroads. The yard was retired after the 1996 merger with Union Pacific. (Mel Lawrence photograph, David M. Bernstein Collection.)

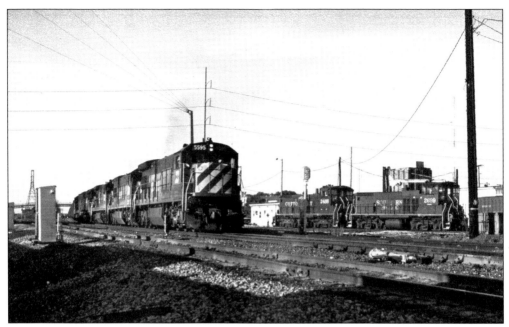

An empty coal train is passing Broadway Yard and entering Tower 55 interlocking on April 29, 1984. The coal was unloaded at the City Public Service generating plant at Elmendorf near San Antonio, and the Southern Pacific crew will interchange the train to the Burlington Northern at North Yard in Fort Worth, who will then take the train to Wyoming to be reloaded. (Jimmy Barlow.)

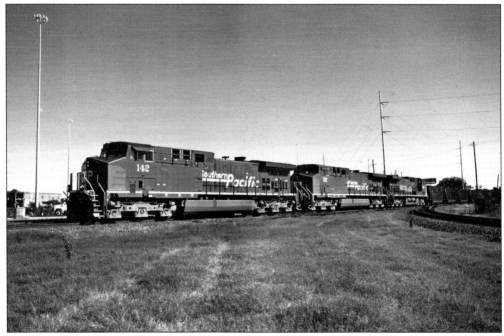

An empty unit coal train is passing through Tower 55 in Fort Worth behind three 4,400-horsepower AC4400CW locomotives in September 1996. The 279 AC4400CW locomotives delivered in 1995 were the last locomotives purchased by Southern Pacific. The train was unloaded at the Central Power & Light generating plant at Coleto Creek near Victoria. (Jimmy Barlow.)

Bibliography

Bernstein, David M. *Corporate History of Southern Pacific Lines in Texas and Louisiana.* Fort Worth, TX: unpublished manuscript in preparation for publication, 2010.
Bernstein, David M. *The Southern Pacific Guide Texas and Louisiana Lines.* Streamwood, IL: Privately published, 1995.
Diebert, Timothy S. and Joseph A. Strapac. *Southern Pacific Company Steam Locomotive Compendium.* Huntington Beach, CA: Shade Tree Books, 1987.
Hofsommer, Don L. *The Southern Pacific: 1901–1985.* College Station, TX: Texas A & M University Press, 1986.
McLennan, A. D. *Texas & New Orleans–Southern Pacific's Lines in Texas and Louisiana.* Wilton, CA: Signature Press, 2008.
Strapac, Joseph A. *Southern Pacific Diesel Locomotive Compendium Volume One.* Bellflower, CA: Shade Tree Books, 2004.
Strapac, Joseph A. *Southern Pacific Diesel Locomotive Compendium Volume Two.* Bellflower, CA: Shade Tree Books, 2007.
Texas Almanac and State Industrial Guide, 1946–1947. Dallas, TX: A. H. Belo Corporation, 1947.

Southern Pacific documents, corporate history files, annual reports, maps, employee timetables, and public timetables in the author's collection were the primary historical references consulted in preparation of this book.

Discover Thousands of Local History Books Featuring Millions of Vintage Images

Arcadia Publishing, the leading local history publisher in the United States, is committed to making history accessible and meaningful through publishing books that celebrate and preserve the heritage of America's people and places.

Find more books like this at
www.arcadiapublishing.com

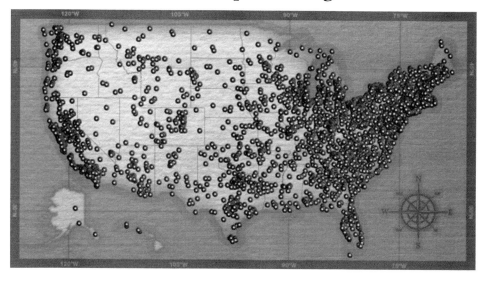

Search for your hometown history, your old stomping grounds, and even your favorite sports team.

Consistent with our mission to preserve history on a local level, this book was printed in South Carolina on American-made paper and manufactured entirely in the United States. Products carrying the accredited Forest Stewardship Council (FSC) label are printed on 100 percent FSC-certified paper.

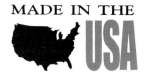